FRESH IMPACT

Mario Murillo

FRESH IMPACT

CREATION
HOUSE
BOOKS ABOUT SPIRIT-LED LIVING
ORLANDO, FLORIDA

Creation House
Strang Communications Company
600 Rinehart Road
Lake Mary, FL 32746
(407) 333-0600
Fax (407) 869-6051

Unless otherwise noted, all Scripture quotations are
from the New King James Version of the Holy Bible.
Copyright © 1979, 1980, 1982 by Thomas Nelson
Inc., publishers. Used by permission.

Scripture quotations marked NIV are from the Holy
Bible, New International Version. Copyright © 1973,
1978, 1984, International Bible Society.
Used by permission.

CONTENTS

Section Three
First the Church, Then the World

FOREWORD

John Wesley once said, "Get on fire for God, and people will come and watch you burn." *Fresh Impact* is a message from a man on fire!

It is indeed an honor and privilege to write the foreword to Mario's new book. I have been a friend of his for many years. His tenacity and toughness to push through hard times speaks to me that he's not only telling us what to do, he is already doing it himself. His ministry has challenged and changed many at Faith Fellowship Ministries as well as others around the world.

I know the man, so it makes his message even more effective to me. In a time where the message of doom seems to be popular, he has announced to a sometimes prayerless, powerless and passionless church that we truly *did* receive power after the Holy Spirit came upon us and that we can and will impact our generation.

Mario's new book can be described as *profound, prolific* and *prophetic: profound,* because although capturing simple truths, it is marked by intellectual depth and insight; *prolific,* because grasping the depth of the truth will certainly produce an abundance of fruit; and *prophetic,* because it is a revelation and prediction of what we can expect if we obey God and what we can expect if we disobey God!

For many years Mario's ministry has been on the cutting edge of the fresh move of God in our nation. His direct, honest and anointed delivery has shaken the religious system of America. God has used him to bring many to tears and many to their knees as they recognize how far we have moved from God and the mainstream of His blessings in our land.

This book will stir your mind and heart to take inventory of where you are spiritually. You will refocus your attention on the important things ahead for the church as we approach the dawning of a new spiritual age. *Fresh Impact* is a book preparing us for a mighty move of the Holy Spirit as promised in the Word of God. It is a voice crying in the wilderness, "Prepare ye the way of the Lord...."

Someone once told me, "Don't determine a man's ministry by how he preaches, but by what trail he leaves behind him." Mario's ministry has been a testimony that wherever he goes he leaves behind him the fresh fragrance of a new wind blowing. The passion, power, fervor and frankness of his message are again captured in writing. The reader will never be the same. He will be challenged; he will be stirred; he will be changed.

Evidences of the ministry God has entrusted to Mario are all over this land: the thousands of souls saved, the hundreds of churches revived and the lives of believers that have been touched to move ahead in faith and integrity for God. This new insight, *Fresh Impact,* is yet another "trail" of the anointing of God in Mario's life.

Thanks, Mario, you did it again, and we are grateful to God for your obedience to be bold and honest. I am sure this is just the beginning of what God is not only doing in you but in all of us!

David T. Demola
Pastor, Faith Fellowship Ministries
  World Outreach Center
Edison, New Jersey
October 6, 1994

FIRE, IMPACT AND YOU

Once a man wanted to cut a lot of firewood. The salesman at the hardware store suggested that he use a chain saw. With a chain saw, the salesman assured him, he could cut several cords of wood at a time.

The next day the man returned to the store, angry and disgusted. "This saw is no good at all. It's heavy, and all I could cut were two small logs!"

The salesman picked up the chain saw to see what was wrong. When the salesman pulled the starter cord, the chain saw roared to life. The man asked, "What's that noise?"

This book is about that noise. We, as Spirit-filled Christians in the time of our nation's greatest darkness, are a great unstarted chain saw.

Something radical has to happen to our nation.

When I wrote *Fresh Fire*, I was concerned that many would consider it too radical. Instead it was devoured by people all over the world. There is a vast hunger for the simple truth of *Fresh Fire*. Don't settle for just one baptism of power during your life; several drenchings must follow. Whenever evil mires the work of God, when our flesh reasserts its corruptions, and when we need wisdom, we can return and ask again for fresh fire.

You must have fresh fire to understand *Fresh Impact*. The power of fresh fire that falls on you inflames you to go and do unimaginable exploits. Fresh impact is all of those great exploits — and their effects.

Think of fresh fire as the fuel and the roaring engine. Think of fresh impact as those razor-sharp chain-saw teeth cutting through evil faster and deeper than you ever imagined possible.

The Bible records example after example of power falling on seemingly insignificant lives. These people were revolutionized beyond their natural limits. They also received something else — an amazing skill and strategy that brought devastation to the works of darkness.

Moses, Samson, Gideon, David and Paul all took fresh fire to a fresh impact.

All of us agree that something radical has to happen to our nation. Our tragedy is classic. The world believes a lie because Hollywood and the news media have stepped way beyond their rightful place. They have an agenda and the resources to carry out that agenda. With their talent they take the foolish, the vile and the empty and make it awesomely appealing, while we take unspeakable glory and a manifold cure and bungle our presentation as if we were lying.

The world lies well, and we tell the truth badly. But I am convinced that we are destined to have a fresh impact, an impact that marshals all of the gifts of power and wisdom through all of God's people everywhere.

How does fresh impact begin? By the reanimation of individual believers — namely you!

We must be weaned from irrelevant charismatic trappings. We must not get our thrills from silly war games. We will never be happy until we drop lesser goals and get fire; then we'll go on to the impact God has marked out for our lives.

I want you to understand the words I use in *Fresh Impact*, not because they are complicated words, but because I use them in a unique way.

- Fresh fire — a new drenching of Holy Spirit power that fuels great exploits.
- Fresh impact — the exploits themselves; your private effect on evil and the effectiveness you were meant to have.
- *Dunamis* — the power of God that renders you effective.

My great passion in writing this book is to take people out of harmless, insignificant lives they have no business living and bring them into lives of impact.

Not only is our nation redeemable, but it can become a greater nation than it has ever been. The key is a new breed of Spirit-filled Christians, and it begins with a deep and sincere cry: "Jesus, I want to be a fresh impact!"

GETTING READY

ONE

WAKE UP AND SELL THE COFFIN!

Let me ask you something you are not asked every day: Are you a walking dead person? By this I mean to say that, even though you are breathing, has the real life you were meant to live ceased?

Living dead people are everywhere. At some point their dreams, visions and zeal were extinguished, and a lower form of living began. Their body language reveals them. They carry the manner-isms of people doing time. They have a condition worse than low self-esteem. It is low life-esteem.

The living dead exist in coffins nicely decorated to deflect the image of death. These caskets may be the secure routines we've chosen in lieu of true destinies. They may be the practical and realis-

Being in the center of God's purpose for your life is the safest place there is.

tic living which has doused our original fire. Anything in which you hide, anything that kills the real you, is a coffin.

When you rehash your life in the still of the night, do you feel the pain of compromise? Do you feel the weight of the life you might have led?

Fresh impact is not about lashing out at hyp-ocrites; it is about the amazing effect Spirit-filled Christians are supposed to have but don't. It's time to wake up and sell the coffins!

The charismatic movement is now virtually a car-icature of its own message. We have shout but no clout. We claim authority but have taken no mean-ingful ground. We write songs of victory over evil that are suitable for the playground, not the battleground.

When you are baptized in the Holy Spirit, your capacity for a life of power takes a quantum leap. But if you retreat after receiving power, your capac-ity for misery increases just as dramatically.

We get frustrated and tired. We lash out at people we love with an anger we don't understand. Our near-death life allows us to form alliances with shady people. We discard joy and love for jaded survival instincts.

How does this happen? First look at the toxic end-times heart condition that noted eighteenth-century theologian Matthew Henry predicted: "We must take heed lest our hearts be overcharged lest they be burdened and overloaded and so unfitted and disabled to do what must be done."[1]

Henry goes on to describe the righteous surrounded by a sensual and security-seeking generation. "The immoderate use of meat and drink which burden the heart not only with the guilt thereby contracted but by the ill influence which such disorders of the body have upon the mind; they make men dull and lifeless to their duty, dead and listless in their duty; they stupefy the conscience, and cause the mind to be unaffected with those things which are most affecting.

"The inordinate pursuit of the good things of this world overcharges the heart with the cares of this life."[2]

No one can answer for you; you must be honest. Did the multiple warhead of fear, disappointment and sensual distraction cause you to abandon your destiny? Were you crushed and embittered by disappointment, accepting an unfit and disabled life?

I remember my first brush with death. It was at

a meeting with my high school counselor. I was born again too late to save my grades! My counselor told me that my 1.9 grade point average proved I wasn't college material.

Look at death closely! Though I knew inside myself that I was supposed to brave the academic world, the counselor's advice to me was to enter a trade school and learn manual labor.

I felt the tentacles of fear that drive people to overdependency on government social programs. I was frightened by college and strangely drawn to the security (remember this word) of government protection.

Members of minorities sometimes catch — on the edge of a remark or in unspoken sympathy — a sense that they are victims. It's the "we will take care of you" attitude. That's how I felt just then. At stake, in that moment, was my whole future: my calling, my destiny, the miracle of worldwide witness!

When you rehash your life in the still of the night, do you feel the pain of compromise?

All the undergrowth of my ghetto experience was telling me to get in the coffin.

One thing I learned that day was that when you get filled with the Holy Spirit, you lose your right to choose when the power may fall on you! Right there and then the Spirit rose in me like a volcano. I shouted at the top of my lungs, "I can do all things through Christ who strengthens me!"

I fled the counselor's lair and enrolled in college. Not only did I enroll, but I chose challenging courses — psychology, sociology, political science. My grade point average that first year was a 3.5.

Security: A Substitute for Destiny

Something very sophisticated, evil, powerful and unrelenting is conspiring to get you to accept a deadly substitute for your destiny. Using our hardened and poisoned times, this monster seeks to place you in a box — not to get you to backslide (that's too obvious), but to get you to live symbolically instead of actually, to have "a form of godliness" but denying the impact of it (see 2 Tim. 3:5).

"We cannot be safe so long as we are secure," said Matthew Henry.[3] So what is the difference between safety and security? Security is the demented pursuit of all things that remove uncertainty. It is an end-times obsession. Security offers you food and shelter in exchange for your freedom.

When you subconsciously decide that our nation is unchangeable; that your little life cannot make a difference; that your dream just takes too much out of you; then you end up in the prison of security.

Safety, on the other hand, is peace through victory. It is placing your life at divine risk; choosing to find and fulfill the purpose of your life. Being in the center of God's purpose for your life is the safest place there is.

It's time to wake up and sell the coffin! It is quite possible that you are not at all who you think you are, nor are you doing what you were meant to do. This means you may need to be blown out of the tomb of a nonimpact life.

Arising to Fresh Impact

If ever I found this to be true, it was early in my ministry when death came calling again. I was preaching in a little church in Chico, California, to a crowd of twenty-five people, mostly senior citizens. They were all Christians, and this made it especially difficult since I was trying to be a soul-winner.

> *When you are baptized in the Holy Spirit, your capacity for a life of power takes a quantum leap.*

It got so bad that on the final night I preached I made a rash vow to God. If a soul was not saved that night I would leave the ministry! To reinforce to God how serious I was, I found a job that would begin the next morning.

All that day I prayed. I prayed everything I knew to pray. When I finally arrived at the little church, I saw the most discouraging sight of my life — a meager crowd who I knew were all Christians. My

21

ministry was over. That service was a tedious and painful exercise that moved as slow as a glacier.

When the ordeal finally ended, I drove back to the hotel at the Christian conference center where I was staying. It was raining so hard I could barely see the road. My first thought was how appropriate the rain was for such a dark and sad moment in my life.

My hotel room had to be the loneliest place on earth. My heart was so broken I was beyond tears. I got ready for bed knowing I had to be at work early the next morning. I lay there and realized how badly I wanted to be a preacher — and now it would never happen.

The phone rang. The voice I heard was the last voice on earth I ever expected to hear. It was John, a high school classmate. John was, well, a "jerk" in high school, so I knew this had to be Satan adding insult to injury.

My shock intensified when he said, "Mario, I've been saved!" But what he said next was beyond amazing.

Somehow John had heard that I was in this hotel. He was now a leader in the California youth prison system. He had seventy-five delinquent drug abusers at a retreat in the same hotel where I was staying. He called me from the lobby and said that the speaker they had scheduled was unable to come because the roads were washed out. My car had been the last one to make it through before the flooding began. John needed a preacher and told me, "I know you are supposed to speak to these young men."

How can I describe to you the joy and power

that rose in me at that moment? I sailed down to the lobby and broke into their meeting. Fire came over me. All of them were saved after I preached! But I could not leave it there. I prayed, and each one received the baptism in the Holy Spirit.

As surely as Lazarus rose from the dead, I was resurrected to my assigned impact. I had been dead to my destiny and didn't even know it.

This book can show you how to find your personal fresh impact. If you have bought the lie that you can't be equipped to devastate evil and have a powerful impact, then wake up and sell the coffin! If you have assumed that our nation is beyond hope and charismatics can't bring lasting moral change, then wake up and sell the coffin!

There are enemies of impact, and I am determined to expose them one by one. But the fresh impact begins by a violent renouncing of that life into which Satan has boxed you.

Do not read this with

Something very sophisticated, evil, powerful and unrelenting is conspiring to get you to accept a deadly substitute for your destiny.

eyes glazed over by cynicism. Do not read this with a hard heart. *Fresh Impact* will be either a block of wood or a living book that launches you into an indescribable new world that is waiting for your arrival.

TWO

WE ARE NOT SUPPOSED TO LEAVE QUIETLY

I have this feeling about you. I believe you are about to embrace a life of emotional and spiritual effectiveness that is greater than you ever imagined.

Why do I believe this? Chiefly because you chose to read this book (or perhaps you were chosen to read this book). You see, I have prayed for the Holy Spirit to place this work into the right hands. So I have this conviction that you are not like most people on this planet. You have a passion to live a life of impact!

If you will allow me to walk you through the real meaning of fresh impact, I believe your gravest doubts and deepest frustrations will melt before the fire of a new life. Think about it! Throughout time there have been heroes of faith whose impact could not be explained by their talent or popularity. Their very lives were the impact.

A Life of Impact

Look at these descriptions to see the power Samuel's life commanded:

> So Samuel grew, and the Lord was with him and let none of his words fall to the ground (1 Sam. 3:19).
>
> So the Philistines were subdued, and they did not come anymore into the territory of Israel. And the hand of the Lord was against the Philistines all the days of Samuel (1 Sam. 7:13).

Daniel was another whose powerful life forced changes by simply being present.

> Then this Daniel distinguished himself above the governors and satraps, because an excellent spirit was in him; and the king

gave thought to setting him over the whole realm (Dan. 6:3).

By contrast, we charismatics — numbering in the millions — have been unable to force many changes in mainstream America.

But what about our brash outbursts about authority over Satan? What about our war dances and militant lyrics? Do any of these really impact our society?

A Drought of Impact

Often, instead of seeking impact, desperate preachers revise facts, bend purposes and cheer people on to hollow victory. Religious entertainers mask themselves as prophets and suspend their groupies in a state of "Spirit-filled" virtual reality.

Christian gatherings of these people who deny God's power use emotion to celebrate nonsense and try to make the trivial urgent. So slick are these theological engineers that if any of them were the captain of the Titanic, they would announce, "We've only stopped to get ice."

Let's face it: Our nation is not a Christian nation. There are as many children in America that are shot and killed or sexually molested as there are in any other place on earth. What is happening in Los Angeles is an omen of what is to come to every major city. The Southern California gangs are a festering cancer of youth rage. They carry automatic weapons and vastly outnumber the police.

Meanwhile, our country is so open-minded that our brains have fallen out. A majority favor abortion, the normalization of homosexuality and increased restrictions on churches. We are now more pagan, violent, atheistic and anti-Bible than many of the countries where we send missionaries.

It is false comfort to speak of church growth. During this drought of impact, mega-churches tend to empty out little ones. There is more marketing than miracles, more relocation than reproduction, more convenience than conversion.

No matter how mighty the church services seem, we still scurry back to a world reeling with bloodshed, perversion and fear, and we still have to send children to godless schools.

No matter how "big" we look in the sanctuary, we still are dropping in numbers overall. Consider this sobering statistic: New Age has become one of the fastest growing spiritual movements in history. In many areas New Agers greatly outnumber charismatics.

What happened to our impact? Where is our authority over evil? Where is God's steel punch through yielded soldiers? When will we see breakthroughs where it really matters?

The answer, I believe, begins with this declaration: We are not supposed to leave quietly. What does that mean? To find out, let's journey back to an event recorded in Acts 16.

Forcing a Verdict

It's midnight in the lonely Philippian jail. Paul and Silas could have justified having the ultimate pity party. They saw a vision and knew that God wanted them in Philippi. All they were doing was obeying God. They had just commanded one spirit to leave a young girl when — wham! — they were arrested and placed in stocks in the inner prison.

Whenever evil encroaches and the work of God is thwarted, God longs to send fresh fire.

But instead of succumbing to despair, they sang songs to God at midnight.

Here we see the first step to a life that does not leave quietly. By worshipping the Lord, Paul and Silas positioned themselves for God's intervention. Moreover, they were declaring God's goodness regardless of their situation. Their panic was suppressed, and in rushed the Holy Spirit's presence. They lived up to the reputation of their ancestor Joshua — they raised their voices, and the whole jail collapsed! Their singing literally brought down the house, because God sent an earthquake.

This was no ordinary earthquake; it made a statement. All the chains broke, and the doors opened.

It is fascinating how politicians can be counted on to have the most absurd reactions to crises. Those who had ordered Paul and Silas into prison sent word back to Paul and Silas through a messenger saying they were free to go now and to leave quietly. Only politicians could be so naive as to think they had any authority to release men whose singing just leveled the jailhouse!

Can you hear this philosophy echoed in the haunting refrain of liberal politicians? They are telling the church to bow out gracefully. They say we are intruders, and they promise not to hurt us if we keep the gospel a safe distance from secular society.

Remember I told you that the earthquake made a statement? Listen carefully. This is at the heart of impact: It is the solemn duty of a vessel of God to enforce the statement that a miracle is trying to make.

Miracles are vulnerable; Satan can obscure or distort them. It takes courage to seize an act of God and force a verdict in the mainstream culture.

In my book *Fresh Fire* I addressed the problem with receiving only one baptism of power in your life. Whenever evil encroaches and the work of God is thwarted, God longs to send fresh fire to launch a new offensive. Fresh impact is that offensive. In short, *fresh fire* is renewed power to do something; *fresh impact* is what should be done.

The earthquake at Philippi is our model of fresh fire. Here was a loud explosion that tore away the enemy's muzzle on the gospel. Paul could have left quietly. To save his neck he could have justified a polite P.R. exit, but he knew better. He knew his key role was to verify what God was saying through this earthquake.

So this man of God went into a righteous rage. He reiterated their evil to them:

> But Paul said to them, "They have beaten us openly, uncondemned Romans, and have thrown us into prison. And now do they put us out secretly? No indeed! Let them come themselves and get us out" (Acts 16:37).

Paul demanded a parade!

This strikes at the heart of a widespread attitude. Do we subconsciously nurse the idea that we have no right to order civic leaders around or to demand due process or to intrude on our nation's lifestyle even when the fire of God has come and seeks to fuel an impact?

How many of our mass get-togethers — where we safely practiced miracles — dissipated, when instead cities might have been transformed if only we had discerned the next step?

When government writes a law that persecutes the church, we cannot leave quietly. When Satan bribes us with safe passage, we cannot go in peace. When power comes and opportunity knocks, we cannot run for cover.

Paul made his demands clear, and the city fathers

caved in. That's impact! They were forced to connect the earthquake with the gospel. They escorted the men of God out of the prison, asking them to leave Philippi. Even then Paul did not leave as they wished; he made one last stop to see the brethren at Lydia's house.

Try to imagine yourself as one of the first converts of the Philippian church. No sooner are you converted than your movement is driven underground. You might ask yourself, Am I nuts? Why did I join a ragtag cult that is now illegal?

This trembling, fledgling little band knew Paul was in prison, and maybe they were thinking that they would be next. Then came a knock at the door. They answered it reluctantly. There before their eyes were the two beaming apostles, having just left a cowering city council! Paul gave these converts proof of the surpassing power of their faith. He must have unleashed one awesome message of encouragement!

Do you feel the rumbling of unused gifts yearning to find expression? Like Paul, you can be given a focused strategy.

These Christians had not put their souls in the trust of a zany religion. No, they were members of a movement built on a Rock, and the gates of hell would not prevail against it.

A church seemingly doomed to fail now possessed supernatural confidence. Paul reminded them of this when he later wrote them saying, "He who has begun a good work in you will complete it until the day of Jesus Christ" (Phil. 1:6).

Now the city had to take the Philippian church seriously.

Enforce the Impact

Today's charismatic church is long overdue for impact. We have already received power. Now we must enforce the impact that our miracle has set up.

All around us are examples of how we have abandoned miracles out of fear and ignorance. Do you personally feel the rumbling of unused gifts yearning to find expression? Like Paul, you can be given a focused strategy.

I know fire is within you, raging against the evil around you, but there are forces at work trying to lull you into a quiet exit. The enemy of your soul is trying to soothe the feeling of urgency and console you with safe goals and low-impact living.

Can you look clearly at your own life and see the relationships that feed compromise and dull the edge of your sword?

In the very center of your crisis lies an opportunity. You know there are things you are doing now that are temporary. You are doing them only until you find the thing you really want to do, the real work you were meant to do.

When the fire reaches your core, you will trash all the vestiges of harmless, powerless living.

Say it one last time: "I am not supposed to leave quietly."

THREE

I Go to Repair
a Place for You

The juries at the trials of John and Lorena Bobbitt and the Menendez brothers are trying to tell us something: No one is guilty! John is not guilty of rape. Lorena is not guilty of malicious wounding. Lyle and Erik are not guilty of murdering their parents.

Just as an abundance of lawyers created a lawsuit-happy nation (so many legal mouths to feed), now a bumper crop of therapists is helping millions see themselves as victims. We are a nation basking in newly discovered phobias and syndromes.

The Victim's Theology

The cry of the "abused" is "I can't help myself. I am not responsible."

We are told that it is not our fault if we are messed up. The blame lies within certain behavioral stimuli — Vietnam, childhood trauma, something in the water, genetics, bad karma, hormones or whatever — but not us.

Not only do many "victims" believe they should not be punished, but they insist on punishing people who do not accept them. In Los Angeles a bankrupt businessman sued the bank that lent him millions. Even though the bank lost all that it lended him, the businessman contended that they knew he had a problem handling funds and they therefore contributed to his problem. A 450-pound woman sued McDonald's claiming discrimination — their seats weren't big enough. And, on a much sadder note, a judge in Minnesota acquitted a man who committed a vicious rape, citing his abnormally high level of testosterone.

The ultimate, however, has to be the liberal leader who blamed Ronald Reagan for the AIDS epidemic. He said this crisis was not caused by behavior but by cutting spending for social programs.

It seems that everywhere we look there is a resident behavioral expert ready to decriminalize any defendant.

The victim's movement has a clear goal, and that is to get as many problems as possible reclassified as diseases. As Charles J. Sykes said in his book *A Nation of Victims,* "The modern American culture of the support group grew out of a single epiphany: Once the language of disease and addiction could be applied to *behavior* rather than merely to biological disorders, almost any aspect of human life could be redefined in medical terms."[1] The cry is If a habit can't be broken, don't try to fix it — normalize it!

True victims deserve our complete compassion. But there is no doubt that the psychoanalytical tentacles that seek to decriminalize unlawful and immoral behavior reach way too deep into our culture. In fact, they have slithered into the church with devastating results. We now have a victim theology with its own special breed of ministers.

Look at this excerpt from *A Nation of Victims:*

The following notice was posted in a Colorado church:

SUPPORT GROUPS MEET WEEKLY IN
THE PARISH HOUSE AS FOLLOWS:

Sunday
12:00 M.— Cocaine Anonymous, main floor
5:30 P.M. — Survivors of Incest, main floor

6:00 P.M. — Al-Anon, 2nd floor
6:00 P.M. — Alcoholics Anonymous, basement

Monday

5:30 P.M. — Debtors Anonymous, basement
6:30 P.M. — Codependents of Sex Addicts
               Anonymous, 2nd floor
7:00 P.M. — Adult Children of Alcoholics, 2nd
               floor
8:00 P.M. — Alcoholics Anonymous, basement
8:00 P.M. — Al-Anon, 2nd floor
8:00 P.M. — Alateen, basement
8:00 P.M. — Cocaine Anonymous

Tuesday

8:00 P.M. — Survivors of Incest Anonymous,
               basement

Wednesday

5:30 P.M. — Sex & Love Addicts Anonymous,
               basement
7:30 P.M. — Adult Children of Alcoholics, 2nd
               floor
8:00 P.M. — Cocaine Anonymous, main floor

Thursday

7:00 P.M. — Codependents of Sex Addicts
               Anonymous, 2nd floor
7:00 P.M. — Women's Cocaine Anonymous, 2nd
               floor

Friday

5:30 P.M. — Sex & Love Addicts Anonymous,
               basement

    5:45 P.M. — Adult Overeaters Anonymous, main
             floor
    7:30 P.M. — Codependents Anonymous, base-
             ment
    7:30 P.M. — Adult Children of Alcoholics, 2nd
             floor
    8:00 P.M. — Cocaine Anonymous, main floor

Saturday

    10:00 A.M. — Adult Children of Alcoholics,
             main floor
    12:00 M. — Self-Abusers Anonymous, 2nd
             floor[2]

While certain support groups seem to work, we cannot overlook one vital point that contradicts Scripture. In this type of group therapy each member begins by saying, "I am a self-abuser," "I am a sex addict" and so forth.

I am sorry, but I do not think a child of God should stand up and say, "I am an alcoholic," or "I am a cocaine addict," no matter how pervasive these tendencies are in his or her life. The redeemed must say, "I am a new creature in Christ. I am being molded into the image of Jesus. I am complete in Him who is the head of all things." Psalm 107:2 declares, "Let the redeemed of the Lord say so."

Therapy advocates will defend this confessing of one's addictions, claiming it breaks denial and gives the self-abuser the harsh dose of reality needed to face the long road to recovery.

I do not disagree that addicts must face their problem. My question is, What do they face it with? I say they must face it with a clear picture of the power of God and the unswerving promise of victory in Jesus!

The answer to a bad past is a Spirit-filled present in which we load up on new behavior that results from having a new identity. Moreover, if we have been redeemed, we must say so, or we are in denial.

All around us we can observe Christians who have postponed life as they binge on self-discovery.

Victim theology has a much broader influence than just support groups. It has diffused into many forms. The pursuit of emotional well-being is its overriding theme, and its effect is pure disaster.

Victim theology has removed the impact of many churches. All around us we can observe Christians who have shut down for repair. They have postponed life as they binge on self-discovery.

Victim theology creates the idea of a lifetime of recovery. We have reduced Jesus to Someone who is, in essence, "repairing" a place for us. And in Christian circles this process can involve nontherapeutic terminology: "I am breaking a generational curse," "I am being cleansed of a spirit of rejection, or demonic low self-esteem."

Greg Laurie, an affiliate pastor of Calvary Chapel in Santa Ana, California, preached on the abuse of demonology, mentioning a man who claimed to have the demon of disco fever. Demons are real, and deliverance is needed in specific cases, but this can also be an excuse for escapism.

How can God field an army as long as we are locked in the barracks of encounter groups?

Am I just carrying out a mean-spirited attack on true victims? Absolutely not. Let's give them all the compassion they need. Instead this is a call to remove a falsehood that blunts our impact.

When these psyche-merchants first belched these ideas onto the church, men and women of God should have exposed their nonbiblical premises. Instead they were embraced and, in some cases, have produced entire congregations led by recovery-oriented pastors.

Pastors who once preached with power now tinker with people's minds, offering monotonous, meandering talks about how we got the way we are and how we are loved just the way we are. Their sheep swoon in a blissful state of repair and marvel at how deeply their pastor understands them.

But a closer look reveals a dark condition. To use some of the recovery movement's lingo, the pastor and congregation have become codependent.

In codependency we find a trade-off of pain and euphoria. There are punishment and pleasure. The pastor punishes the people with a complicated view

40

of themselves. This view weakens them and makes them dependent on their "spiritual counselor." The hearers are consoled and stroked but not held accountable to triumph in Christ. They are free to recuperate, and while they do, they are, of course, in no condition to win others to Christ.

The pastor's pleasure is the people's adoring gaze, the sense of being needed. But this has a terrible price. The pastor lives in dread of displeasing his people; they are weak and will never follow a vision. They have been taught to think always of themselves first, and

We are not the products of what happens to us. We have a say in what adversity does to us.

they enslave the pastor to their inexhaustible need for attention.

Let's imagine what victim theology would have done for Joseph (see Gen. 37–50).

Man's Therapy vs. God's Therapy

Joseph tells his brothers his dream. He describes how they will pay homage to him. In a blind rage they toss him in a pit. This is what you call a dysfunctional family!

Now Joseph is sold into slavery. Much has been made by sociologists of the so-called slave mentality.

This form of low self-esteem foments crime, illegitimate births and unemployment.

Joseph becomes the property of Potiphar. He takes excellent care of the man's home, but Potiphar's wife tries to seduce him. Joseph runs from her, and in her scorn she has him arrested for attempted rape. This blatant miscarriage of justice no doubt caused a persecution complex and paranoia.

In prison Joseph becomes a foreman, a leader. Psychiatrists have isolated a condition in some prisoners-of-war called the Stockholm syndrome in which the victim sympathizes with his captors. This syndrome was used as a defense by Patty Hearst to explain why she helped her kidnappers rob a bank.

Finally Joseph sees his ticket out of the slammer. Two officials of Pharaoh, a baker and a butler, have fallen into disfavor. They are arrested and thrown into prison with Joseph, where they both have dreams. Joseph interprets the dreams and predicts their fates. Then he solemnly charges the butler that, when he is restored to his job, he is to speak to the Pharaoh on Joseph's behalf.

But the butler forgets about Joseph and doesn't fulfill his promise. Joseph surely must have sunk into a depressed state of mind.

Now let's tally up Joseph's emotional baggage. He is depressed, a victim of Stockholm syndrome, a paranoid with a persecution complex and a slave mentality. Plus he's challenged by a dysfunctional family history. Whew!

Surely a lifetime of therapy is called for here. Instead Joseph becomes a man of the ages, a consummate leader and a beacon of wisdom and compassion.

Joseph had "divine Teflon" in his spirit. This should speak to us. We are not the products of what happens to us. We have a say in what adversity does to us.

Joseph isolated the secret of his power when he named his firstborn son Manasseh. The name means "the Lord has caused me to forget."

Fresh impact is our life being rendered effective by the Lord's hand causing us to forget. We do not need to shut down for repairs; we need to let God "shut up" our past.

Honestly, who is truly qualified to be used of God? None of us! And to wait until we are sure we are worthy to be used of Him is to sit out life altogether.

This does not mean we are not to be holy. People who have God's hand on them will seek to be pure and will always pursue a higher plane. Yes, there are also key times when we must pull away and sharpen the axe. But we must not make a life of it.

Healed As You Go

In another biblical example we read in Mark 16 about what Jesus' disciples did after He had been crucified: They were holed up having a private pity party.

This meeting of Disciples Anonymous was crashed by the appearance of the resurrected Christ Himself! Instead of consolation, Christ delivered the sternest rebuke they had ever received:

> Later He appeared to the eleven as they sat at the table; and He rebuked their unbelief and hardness of heart, because they did not believe those who had seen Him after He had risen (Mark 16:14).

These disciples were guilty of three serious sins:

1. Doubting three and a half years of warning and training about His crucifixion and resurrection.
2. Dismissing the accounts of those who had reported His resurrection.
3. Hard-heartedness.

Surely these character flaws meant they were unfit for service. But to their utter astonishment they were not even placed on probation. With His next breath Jesus said,

> Go into all the world and preach the gospel to every creature. He who believes and is baptized will be saved; but he who does not believe will be condemned.
> And these signs will follow those who

believe. In My name they will cast out demons; they will speak with new tongues; they will take up serpents; and if they drink anything deadly, it will by no means hurt them; they will lay hands on the sick, and they will recover (Mark 16:15-18).

The Holy Spirit would get around to correcting the carnality of these apostles, but the point was that they be healed as they went. Being healed as you go is a central key to fresh impact.

What would really scare Satan? To see the church shift from repairing to reloading!

Doctors now concede that early on polio victims were given bad advice when they were told to stay off the diseased leg. This turned out to encourage deterioration. "Get up and use it," they would now say.

Hebrews applies this advice so clearly:

Therefore strengthen the hands which hang down, and the feeble knees, and make straight paths for your feet, so that what is lame may not be dislocated, but rather be healed (Heb. 12:12-13).

Don't get off your feet and sit it out; make straight paths so that you may be healed.

45

Yes, there are moral failures that demand a halt to ministry until true repentance and restoration are completed. And we must have times of getting away to sharpen our swords. But the psycho-emotional fog that many are wandering in is a satanic distraction meant to keep their weapons silent and their impact non-existent.

If you wait until you feel ready to be used by God, forget it. That day will not come. If you feel you have failed Jesus so deeply that you can't ever be useful again, then how do you explain the tremors of gifts yearning to come out of you?

If the Holy Spirit is quickening you, then who can speak against it? Not Pharisees or therapists; not even you can speak against the voice of God telling you to get up and go do it!

Do you want to know what would really scare Satan? To see the church shift from repairing to reloading!

FOUR

DOUBTFIRE

Imagine yourself the general of a vast army. It is the eve of battle. You are about to put thousands of young lives in harm's way. What should be your gravest concern? Weapons, tactics, troop morale? The voices of ancient warriors echo a warning: Beware of the classic error of war — a mistake so obvious and basic it is easily overlooked. This blunder has lost the war for every army that has committed it.

What is this fatal error? Not knowing your objective.

What Is Your Objective?

It sounds silly, but it's true. Great battalions have gone out to fight with everything but the one thing that mattered most — a clear definition of victory.

In war you must first visualize the desired result of your fighting. Because victory will mean something unique in each case, it is vital that you choose the right objective — and that your objective is clearly communicated to every soldier.

Every fighter in your regiment should be able to recite and answer these questions: What am I going to do once we start fighting? What is the goal of my combat?

Why is defeat so certain without a statement of mission? For openers, it is your objective that should create your strategy and tactics.

Armies put their best military minds to work to forge their definition of victory. This objective is nailed down by combining accurate information about both themselves and their enemy. Once they know the exact conditions that define victory, they can work backward to choose the best strategy to win.

An army can look formidable and be loaded with tactics, but what if the tactics are wrong for this war, useless against this adversary?

Are We Winning — or Just Busy Losing?

Fighting with no stated goal can also lead to a war of attrition — a slow defeat in which you actually seem to be winning. What you are busy doing looks right and brings results, but you can't see the long-range damage your results are masking. You can't see that what you are doing cannot take you where you really want to go. Eventually your army will atrophy.

An objective would *Your objective* expose this false success. It *should create* would be a compass to help *your strategy* you stay on the course, a *and tactics.* gauge to judge actions versus distractions. With it an army can declare, "No matter how good this action looks, it violates our objective."

The greatest war of attrition recently waged was the Vietnam War. The objective was murky and kept changing. It was kicked back and forth between the Pentagon and politicians, and America took years to realize it had lost the war and sacrificed so much for almost nothing.

Israel was solemnly warned not to make covenants with the kings they deposed. This would distract them from their goal — full possession of the land (see Deut. 7:1-5). But taking captives as slaves and demanding tributes were a natural part of ancient war, so Israel decided to do it too. It seemed

right. This became a snare that delayed their possession of the promised land. They took their sight off
their objective and busied themselves with activity
that looked right in their own eyes.

Doubtfire is what I call all the activity that we,
the Spirit-filled church, are excitedly doing, but
which violates our Holy Spirit-given objective.

We do so much that seems right, and it's not really
wrong, but it is powerless against our enemy. What
we are busy doing is not able to take us to a win.

Here are four major reasons that mighty armies
have gone to war without a specific goal to win.
Look at them and see if you notice a spooky comparison to Spirit-filled ministry today.

1. Their healthy awareness of danger is suppressed by past victory and overconfidence.
2. They have sentimental attachment to tactics
   that are out of touch with the current threat.
3. They trust inaccurate information about
   themselves and their enemy.
4. They assume they have an objective because
   they have everything else (equipment, maps,
   programs, and so on).

These are the factors that created the spiritual
equivalent of Vietnam. Though we have thousands
of churches and have spent millions, we are mired in
a war of attrition. We are losing ground even though
our activity is at an all-time high.

False Substitutes for the True Objective

The worst by-product of aimless combat is inventing objectives in the heat of battle. This is what leaders have done because of panic. Frightened by empty pews, they are racing to find "church growth principles."

Our nation has changed violently in the space of a few decades. Both parents work, leisure time has evaporated, and moral uncertainty has diminished church attendance even among believers. And those

What we are busy doing is not able to take us to a win.

who have leisure time simply want to use it for entertainment.

So some of our doubtfire — activity that doesn't get us to our goal — takes the form of emotional binges meant to draw crowds. Or we use pure entertainment in church as a quick fix.

But by far the most popular trend is a move toward "seeker-friendly services." This approach creates a Sunday worship experience that is nonthreatening and nonconfrontive to someone seeking to know more about God. With drama, multimedia and practical pep talks, the gospel is gently divulged over time to the inquirer.

There is a very compelling argument for this method. It is sensitive to what people feel today. It removes condemning words, religious ritual and terminology that are antiquated or boring and turn off visitors.

In fact, you can't say this approach is wrong since it is bred by a desire to win souls. Yet that is precisely why it is so dangerous. You can't detect its long-range damage until you hold it up against scriptural objectives. The Scriptures call us to escape the corruption of this age *immediately.* "And with many other words he testified and exhorted them saying, 'Be saved from this perverse generation' " (Acts 2:40). The Scriptures call for members of the body of Christ to serve each other — not focus on their own needs.

Preachers can be seduced by what produces numbers, and seeker-friendly services can draw crowds. Yet even in this, as I will show you later, we miss out on real numerical impact.

Being seeker-friendly is permissible to a leader who is unfamiliar with the power of God and has not been birthed in signs and wonders. But I submit to you that once you taste the fire of God, you will implement strategies and objectives that speak from that fire. Everything else is doubtfire.

To be sure, the seeker-friendly trend looks good against failed charismatic binges, but that is not the right comparison. Seeker-friendly evangelism should be compared to the classic awakenings that brought quality and quantity of conversions till cities fell. The reawakening at Azusa Street and the revival in Wales both featured charismatic gifts and brought violent change to masses of people.

Again, I am not saying that being seeker-friendly is wrong. But I am saying it is wrong for a preacher with supernatural roots. The same Holy Spirit that gave you power to witness in the first place must be permitted to give you the tactical objective as well.

Tickling Ears vs. Converting Souls

The leader who opts for doubtfire has to ask himself whether doubtfire masks these dangerous assumptions:

1. The assumption that greater numbers are the top priority.

If numbers are your real concern, then why would you choose a model that produces church growth of maybe 15,000 members, while a Spirit-filled "pray and obey" church has grown to almost 800,000 in South Korea?

2. The assumption that if people don't want to hear it, you should alter your presentation to fit their present interest.

Such "culturally relevant" preaching assumes that if an audience either isn't ready for a message or doesn't want to hear it, then you should change it.

Fresh impact says their lack of interest or desperation is irrelevant because the atmosphere of the Holy Spirit creates the desperation and will break down the stage props of their supposedly content life.

Saul of Tarsus was not converted conveniently.

The light and message of the Damascus Road was the violent opposite extreme of his cultural preference.

Truth is not negotiable. The urgency of the cross cannot be financed into easy payments.

Here's the church's shocking dilemma: What do you say to a generation that is flat wrong — and keep them listening?

Even if our gospel is veiled, it is veiled to those who are perishing, whose minds the god of this age has blinded, who do not believe, lest the light of the gospel of the glory of Christ, who is the image of God, should shine on them (see 2 Cor. 4:3-4).

But the lightning of fresh impact pierces the listener's blindness.

Charismatics must remember that on the day of Pentecost the Holy Spirit sent fire evangelism on unsuspecting and culturally diverse souls. They were not ready, but the fire rendered them ready. They were slashed to the heart!

When Peter and those freshly fired disciples preached, they were living out the Spirit-filled objective commanded by Jesus in Mark 16:15: "Go into all the world and preach." The miracles would follow them.

I'm sorry if this sounds blunt, but our choice is very clear. On the day of Pentecost the crowd cried to the apostles, "Men and brethren, what should we do?" (Acts 2:37). Seeker-friendly preachers ask the audience, "O fickle yuppies, what should we preach?"

3. The assumption that power gifts and exuberant worship have no place on Sunday morning.

Just because miracles have been abused is no license to disobey Scripture, which tells us that tongues, for example, are a sign to the unbeliever (see 1 Cor. 14:22).

A Spirit-filled pastor must ask himself, If signs from God cause souls to be saved, why am I stopping them? Shouldn't I be seeking a balanced expression of power that creates impact instead of emotional extremes?

Truth is not negotiable. The urgency of the cross cannot be financed into easy payments.

And as far as worship is concerned, we need to wake up. Free and holy praise releases a presence of God that filters out the cultural distractions and prepares hearts to receive. This form of doubtfire — loading up a Sunday service with human filler to appease trendy people — is a clear enemy of impact.

Relying on the Holy Spirit for Impact

Have you concluded the church's deep need yet? Its deep need is for impact catalyzed by reliance on Holy Spirit objectives.

How I yearn for a church model of fresh impact here at home. We need a body of believers with thirty thousand members who "come short in no gift" (1 Cor. 1:7) and who surrender the whole program to supernatural wisdom. Numbers like these — brought into church by the Holy Spirit — may be the only thing that will jolt many of today's pastors away from marketing fads.

What are we waiting for? Anyone can copy programs. Why use doubtfire when a Jesus objective is available and able to avail?

We can have the Sunday morning that has it all! Worship that blasts lost people to Christ, preaching that pierces instead of appeases, and converts who serve instead of swoon. The church should be a Holy Ghost-designer cure. A mighty pastor hears the overall strategy and thunders it to his charges. They, in turn, apply the impact to the specific hurts of the community.

The focus turns from self-absorption to impact on the children, youth and elderly — in short, the entire spectrum of the need around them. The Sunday morning army should be a veritable seething mass of Spirit-filled, hurt-seeking missiles.

Let's give the Holy Spirit charge in our churches. And, believe it or not, our nation is ready for the same tough preaching, the same radical message of Christ that Peter delivered on the day of Pentecost. In fact, they are longing for it.

FIVE

Doing What Doesn't Work Where It Doesn't Matter

Look carefully. Maybe you can see what I see: the outline of an impact that should be happening but isn't.

On one hand you can see a wicked void in our people, and on the other hand you can see how precisely a Spirit-filled witness would fill that void.

This scenario is my deepest frustration and has become the great passion of my life. How do we put this abundant life into the soul of our nation, whose people, if they only knew it, would find in our message everything they have ever wanted?

A Spiritual Vacuum

There is a God-shaped hole in our society, and we face a choice: to let her dark and godless countenance repulse us or to look deeper and see her overwhelming susceptibility to what we offer.

What we have here is an extreme contrast: a vacuum of peace, love, joy and power in our citizens — and an immeasurable reservoir of all they yearn for in Christ. Just a thin, fragile wall separates a love-starved generation and the God who is more than enough. At some point something has to give.

Just before Hurricane Andrew hit, experts said it would probably carry the most violent winds in history. They based their prediction on the simple fact that the air pressure off the coast of Florida was the lowest ever recorded.

Likewise, we now have the lowest "spiritual air pressure" ever. Our youth have less God influence than any other generation in American history. The wholesale erasure of moral concepts has left a barren, empty-hearted culture. Such an extreme condition portends a convulsive correction.

Perhaps charismatics are living in the luxury of our nation's ignorance about what we truly represent. But this vacation will not last. The weather report of the spirit world warns us — and history warns us.

At key times in history a flat-footed church society has been overrun by masses whose collective eyes were opened. These awakenings cared nothing for how prepared Christians were to handle the throngs.

Of all the spiritual hurricanes of history, surely one of the most underrated was the one touched off by the preaching of John the Baptist. Judea reeled under the twin tragedies of dead religion and Roman occupation. Here was a pure, satanic recipe for damnation. First the devil seduced Pharisees to put layers of technicalities between hungry souls and God, then he ground the people in the crucible of daily oppression.

Yet John's righteous rampage saw masses of people baptized.

> Then Jerusalem, all Judea, and all the region around the Jordan went out to him and were baptized by him in the Jordan, confessing their sins (Matt. 3:5-6).

The truly stunning part was the profound change in the people who thrived under hard preaching. The dumbfounded Pharisees sought an explanation for this typhoon of truth. Jesus explained, "And from the days of John the Baptist until now the kingdom of heaven suffers violence, and the violent take it by force" (Matt. 11:12).

John the Baptist, a true awakener, preached down the wall that separated the kingdom from vacuous hearts.

Lucifer knows he is always in a race against revival. His only hope is to plunge a generation as deep into addictions and perversions as possible to put them beyond conviction. John thundered the kingdom of God, and all of Satan's acts backfired. What Satan meant for damnation became a flash point for God, and multitudes raced to John.

Our adversary is at work again seducing charismatic Christians to speak what doesn't work where it doesn't matter, all the while making our country a concentration camp of dead dreams and abandoned hope. Satan is racing against our impact potential. His hope, as always, is to make this generation reprobate.

Directives for Impacting Society

It is time for you and me to visit another jail in the book of Acts. This account (in Acts 5) will show you the drastic measures the Lord is willing to take to make sure fresh fire becomes fresh impact.

> And [the high priest and Sadducees] laid their hands on the apostles and put them in the common prison (Acts 5:18).

Here is the only time that all the apostles were in

jail together. The devil must have thought he pulled off the greatest coup of all time, but once again he had merely been fooled into making a huge mistake.

Why was this mass arrest such a tactical error? First, it brought them all together. Then, as now, leaders are almost impossible to get together. Once leaders are together (especially if they are fearing for their lives), they tend to resolve differences and remember what is really important.

Now the apostles could hear from God without distraction. They were forced to attend a Bible conference behind bars, and the keynote speaker was an angel of God. This messenger from God delivered a terse but timeless command which held three key directives. These directives are loaded with power, and they speak with surgical accuracy to us today.

Go, stand in the temple and speak to the people all the words of this life (Acts 5:20).

1. Stand together.

By telling them to go, the angel was telling the apostles to take a stand together. Jail had reduced them to their lowest common denominator. They were in it together, and they faced a common threat. Therefore they knew they must take a stand together, and this stand reaffirmed the only objective that could win the war — unity.

The division between leaders today is the worst I have ever seen. It is sickening and, when spiritualized, becomes unbearable. Standing together means you pool your talents to birth a concerted effort. Standing together means no one is dispensable, and when one hurts, all hurt.

The angel was ordering the apostles to drop sectarian attitudes. Have you seen the advancement of cults? Why are their tentacles everywhere? Because they stand together.

You do not see a Jehovah's Witness preacher attack one of his own. Mormon leaders do not take their family fights to the media. New Agers do not assassinate one another's characters. The Christian family is an embarrassing nest of heresy hunters and gossipers in which the morbid pastime is watching leaders fall and then rehashing gory details.

You and I both know of divisive voices in the church who could use a visit to the jail and a lecture from an angel! The agenda for impact comes to those who stand together.

2. Go to the temple.

This is a command to do what works where it matters most. The directive is to go mainstream, go where ideas and trends are created.

The temple was the most visible building in town. What happened there impacted the whole city. What was done there made a difference. This is a rebuke to all of our "secret societies" where we meet and merely fantasize about impact. A secret society is any charismatic group that consciously or unconsciously hides its cure.

It is not amazing to build a church of a few thousand people. What is amazing is how we can contain our impact so completely. How can two thousand people who believe they are awesome beings of authority against Satan meet together and scurry home again without causing a ripple?

How can people who believe they have awesome authority against Satan meet and scurry home again without causing a ripple?

We must put the miracle in the mainstream. Spirit-filled leaders must stand together in the temples of visibility of our nation and let the collision begin! Temples of visibility are the places of public forums. The Jewish temple was the focal point of social and spiritual influence. In our culture it is television, shopping malls, convention centers or any place where opinion is communicated.

3. Tell all the words of this life!

Once I was asked at a junior high camp to temper my preaching. The camp leaders thought the raw power of God was too intense for such young minds. Instead I looked at my preteen audience and announced to them that Satan believed they were now old enough to lose their virginity, and if Satan believed that, then they were also old enough to receive power — Holy Ghost power to help them keep their virginity.

I said, "Satan sees you as old enough to be drug addicts, and if you can be addicted to drugs, you can be addicted to Jesus!"

You can imagine what that angel would think of those who would dilute the gospel!

Since the devil pours all of his vileness onto unwary souls, so must we pour in all the healing properties of the gospel. The oppressed must hear all the words of this life. For multiple hurts we must preach multiple miracles.

To withhold any facet of the good news is treason against the kingdom; it is a crime to the victims of evil, and above all, it is an affront to the suffering of Jesus on the cross. He paid for every benefit. How can we leave any out?

The angel's command to "tell all" nullified any opinion the apostles had about what their culture was ready to hear.

But telling "all the words of this life" means something more, something we just can't seem to get right. We need to do all the things that would create impact. Yet we always end up harping on just one doctrine or gift.

For example, we have churches known for teaching, others known for worship and still others known for outreach. Few, if any, are known for having all of the above. Yet telling all means demonstrating the full counsel of God.

The church of impact has worship, teaching, outreach and an agenda for impact in the mainstream. A Spirit-filled impact church is a center where it is vital to put every aspect of a move of God into action and in its proper place.

Even if the church groupies fall in love with an emphasis, the apostolic leader must enforce the whole symphony of God's design, because then and only then will impact come.

Frenzied crowds are not fresh impact. Someone once asked my opinion of "laughing crusades," as he dubbed them. He told me he didn't think they were real acts of God. I said they were, but they could be orphaned from their real impact if they were not combined with all the other gifts that were supposed to be expressed in the service.

A crusade must include many weapons. While we may have a rollicking good time, a broken life may go untouched because the gift that corresponds to that need — and which might have delivered the one in need — was never expressed.

It is not hard to admit! If what we have been doing could work, it would have worked by now. But what we do for the most part doesn't work where it doesn't matter.

I solemnly warn you that if ever charismatic Christians learn impact, we will be invaded and taken by force like a food riot during a famine. Now let's get you ready to receive that impact in your own life.

SIX

Before You Ask
for Fresh Impact

By now I hope it is clear to you that God has prewired you to house a gift, a weapon, that corresponds exactly to a current evil. What are current evils? Victimized children, lost youth, sexual perversion that goes unchallenged, homelessness or simply the frustating maze of modern life. Not far away a disaster looms, and you are uniquely designed to respond to it!

This revelation is at once thrilling and fearsome — thrilling, because our fresh impact will bring great glory to God and unspeakable joy to us; and fearsome, because what could bring us greater sorrow than to miss our destiny?

In the process of finding your impact you will find yourself, because nothing defines you as completely as your God-given mission. When the time comes that He articulates the race set before you, you will find out more about yourself than you ever imagined.

In finding your impact you will find yourself, because nothing defines you as completely as your God-given mission.

One life is all it takes to start the miracle. Again and again it has happened in history. Seemingly unpromising lives jumped out of obscurity, parted the sea, raised the dead, turned armies to flight and rescued their nation. Now it is your turn to become the dread of demons and a Holy Ghost special effect. Are you ready? Are you serious, or do you still need to take one more lap around a mediocre life?

Do you understand our nation's greatest need? We don't need better buildings or even more Christians but rather mighty acts coming out of buildings we already have and greater impact from believers who are already there.

The moment you ask Jesus to show you, your unique impact will be overpowering. It is one of the most serious requests you will ever make. You cannot do this lightly or double-mindedly. Before you ask for fresh impact, before you seek audience with the Lord, do these things:

1. **Clear your mind.** Silence those negative voices. Forget the cutting remarks of relatives. Dismiss the crippling theories of misguided counselors. Rebuke your self-doubt and turn off the broken record of your past failures. This, my friend, is a new day.

2. **Let God redefine you.** Relinquish to Him your opinion of yourself. Your view no longer matters. He alone decides your true potential.

No matter how compelling your weaknesses, handicaps or acquired phobias seem, they must all be put away. No matter how black tomorrow looks, it is only God who designs your future.

As a youth pastor in Pacifica, California, I saw this miracle of God redefining someone. Many youth had been snatched from a life of drugs there, but one life was particularly lurid. This girl was pretty and seemed innocent, but she had once been a prostitute. The horror of it was that her father was her pimp. Though this girl was now Spirit-filled, she was continually stalked by images of her past. She felt unclean, and she was sinking into despair.

I begged the Lord for an answer for her, and it came, as it so often does, as a simple truth that could easily have been overlooked.

John 16:8 says, "And when He has come, He will convict the world of sin, and of righteousness, and of judgment." There it was! I saw that the Holy Spirit never lets up until we are convinced we are sinners. And this same Spirit also convinces us that we are righteous before God because of Jesus.

I placed my hand on the top of her head and declared to her, "The same Spirit that convinced you of your sin will now convince you that you are cleansed!"

Three days later she returned, exhausted and rejoicing. Every time she tried to rehearse her past, conviction would seize her. She finally wore out and gave in to God's opinion of her. Do the same.

3. Realize that you hear through a filter. There is a major gap between your perception of things and God's perception. How wide is that gap?

> For as the heavens are higher than the earth, so are my ways higher than your ways, and my thoughts than your thoughts (Is. 55:9).

Our grasp of what is going on around us is warped by our episodes of pain — they create filters that muffle what we hear and see. It is this mechanism that causes us to react in ways we don't understand.

Let me offer a vivid example — Gideon. In Judges 6:11 we find him threshing wheat in a winepress out of fear of the Midianites stealing the grain. God sent an angel, who greeted Gideon with these words: "The

Lord is with you, you mighty man of valor!" (v. 12). This was Gideon's fresh impact, his destiny. He would attack and win over the enemy he feared most.

But Gideon was hearing God's message through the filter of his fear. Gideon said to the angel,

> O my lord, if the Lord is with us, why then has all this happened to us? And where are all His miracles which our fathers told us about, saying, "Did not the Lord bring us up from Egypt?" But now the Lord has forsaken us and delivered us into the hands of the Midianites."

In verse 14 God tries again:

> Then the Lord turned to him and said, "Go in this might of yours, and you shall save Israel from the hand of the Midianites. Have I not sent you?"

This time Gideon listens through his inferiority filter and his dysfunctional family filter:

> So he said to Him, "O my Lord, how can I save Israel? Indeed my clan is the weakest in Manasseh, and I am the least in my father's house" (v. 15).

The Lord made a third attempt.

And the Lord said to him, "Surely I will be with you, and you shall defeat the Midianites as one man" (v. 16).

Reluctantly Gideon embraced his destiny.

Your filter will disqualify you; it will mute out any promise or commission from God that exceeds your preconceived limits. This negative cloud will delay and dilute God's voice to you.

To God, Gideon was a mighty man of valor. To himself, Gideon was a nobody from nowhere. Which filters are you hearing God's voice through? Get rid of them before you ask for fresh impact!

You get rid of your filters by exposing them as they occur. Identify past hurts that distort God's messages to you. Try to listen again. Each effort will bring greater clarity and healing. The Word of God is your friend. Each time you rehearse its life-inducing words, another lie will fall away.

4. **Accept that you don't need talent.** Stop and think about it — the most heroic and effective acts of the Bible were exceedingly simple. They required almost no talent. Joshua shouted, Daniel petted lions, Elijah called for fire, Moses raised a rod, and Samson swung a jawbone.

When I am hiring staff, I don't look first for talent. I want someone with loyalty and faithfulness — to which talent can be added. But if someone isn't loyal and faithful, having talent doesn't even matter.

Even Paul said in 1 Timothy 1:12, "And I thank

Christ Jesus our Lord who has enabled me, because He counted me *faithful,* putting me into the ministry" (italics added). We are no different from Paul. We are enabled after we are proven *faithful.*

Do not gauge your impact potential on your present talents. Do not subconsciously disqualify yourself from the messages you hear from God because they exceed your abilities. Whatever God leads you to do carries with it the promise of the necessary skills to do it.

5. Realize that now is the time. To find your impact you must start now. The first step will never be painless, nor the time convenient. Our routines are like terrorists: They make crazy demands, and they won't negotiate.

There will always be some good reason not to block out time to seek fresh impact. Each day brings something urgent to do, an emergency that can't wait. It is amazing, however, how all those things that people convince us we must do have a way of getting done without us.

Forget about waiting for that golden day when the air feels right, the music swells, your ship comes in — and all seems perfect for obtaining fresh impact.

And speaking of perfect, now is a good time to remember the difference between perfectionism and excellence.

Perfectionism is an obsession with waiting to do something until you are positive you can do it perfectly. If perfectionists had developed aviation, we would still be on the ground because they never would have tested an imperfect airplane.

Excellence says, Let's get this thing in the air; let's keep trying until we get it right. Excellence asks, Why isn't right now a good time to start?

Martha complained loudly that her sister, Mary, was not helping her in the kitchen. Jesus corrected her quickly:

> Martha, Martha, you are worried and troubled about many things. But one thing is needed, and Mary has chosen that good part, which will not be taken away from her (Luke 10:41-42).

Likewise for you, only one thing is needed. Choose that good part, and it will not be taken away from you.

It is time to begin. Your destiny is calling. Do you see a local tragedy and the waiting miracle? The only thing that separates the tragedy and the miracle is the lack of an available — not talented — life.

6. Resolve in your heart that fresh impact is not an option. While excellence may help you start, resolution helps you finish.

Cortez was a cruel man, but he had an effective way of convincing his soldiers to conquer the Aztecs after they landed in Mexico. As the men stood at attention on the beach, Cortez ordered the ships burned and sunk. There would be no going back to Spain.

For you this must not be an extracurricular adventure but a harsh reality. Our nation and all we hold dear are threatened. Only a God-sent fire expressed in mass effectiveness can save us now.

Recently I was driving to an inner-city crusade. My driver was a young black professional who had organized the outreach. He told me he was honored that I was willing to come to a troubled area. I said, "This is not an honor for you, nor is it a noble act on my part; it is an urgent necessity."

Then I told him that we all belong to the fire department. If we see a fire, we call the fire department, and when we do that we are helping put out the fire. Likewise, we immediately make way for a screaming fire engine that is racing to a fire.

I told my driver that anyone who would let a fire burn is crazy. "The inner city is on fire," I said. "The hatred, bloodshed and anger are a blaze that will eventually burn down all our nation. I am here to put out this fire before it consumes everyone's house!"

Before you ask for fresh impact, burn the boats that would float you back into a harmless Christian existence.

7. **Understand that you are a part of prophecy.** Look at these five Scripture verses; they are for you.

Arise, shine; for your light has come! And

the glory of the Lord is risen upon you.
For behold, the darkness shall cover the
earth, and deep darkness the people; but
the Lord will arise over you, and His glory
will be seen upon you, the Gentiles shall
come to your light, and kings to the
brightness of your rising (Is. 60:1-3).

And it shall come to pass afterward that I
will pour out My Spirit on all flesh; your
sons and your daughters shall prophesy,
your old men shall dream dreams, your
young men shall see visions (Joel 2:28).

Those who do wickedly against the covenant
he shall corrupt with flattery; but the people
who know their God shall be strong, and
carry out great exploits (Dan. 11:32).

And this gospel of the kingdom will be
preached in all the world as a witness to all
the nations, and then the end will come
(Matt. 24:14).

For the earnest expectation of the creation
eagerly waits for the revealing of the sons
of God. For the creation was subjected to
futility, not willingly, but because of Him
who subjected it in hope; because the creation itself also will be delivered from the

bondage of corruption into the glorious liberty of the children of God (Rom. 8:19-21).

These familiar and intriguing verses, along with many others, present a clear picture of a generation of impact believers who will walk in power during a time of global revelation of God's glory. Moreover, this "army" will come on the scene during the earth's darkest and most wretched hour.

Fresh impact has flared here and there throughout history, but could these prophecies mean that a vast number of lives will express power at the same time? I am convinced this is what is predicted, and I believe you are a part of that prophecy!

Now, as Solomon said, "Let us hear the conclusion of the whole matter" (Eccl. 12:13). You are about to knock on the greatest door in history. On the other side is fresh impact. Have you made yourself ready?

Let me show you how to find out what your fresh impact is.

THE DAY OF POWER:
STEPS TO FRESH IMPACT

SEVEN

STEP 1:

BLOCK OUT A WHOLE DAY TO SEEK FRESH IMPACT

E very mighty vessel of God in history can trace his or her success to a single day of power.

Do not hide Your face from me in the day of my trouble; incline Your ear to me; in the day that I call, answer me speedily. For my days are consumed like smoke, and my bones are burned like a hearth (Ps. 102:2-3).

Moses had his day before a burning bush. David became king in a cave. Esther's day was spent shut up in her chamber. Elijah spent the day on Mt. Carmel bent over with his face between his knees in prayer. Paul had his eyes "opened" while waiting for Ananias.

These men and women emerged from this day devoted to God and knowing their fresh-impact orders — and they went on to change the world.

Even Jesus had days of power. The most notable was in the Garden of Gethsemane. All the steps that lead to fresh impact are vividly portrayed here. He seeks help with an unbridled passion. He rehearses the whole purpose of His life. He asks for the cup to pass but triumphs by declaring "not My will, but Yours, be done" (Luke 22:42). The power to impact had come, and what an impact it was! Colossians 2:15 says, "Having disarmed principalities and powers, He made a public spectacle of them, triumphing over them in it."

What happens when someone blocks out an entire day to seek their destined impact? Let's listen to an angel tell us:

> Then [the angel] said to me, "Do not fear, Daniel, for from the first day that you set your heart to understand, and to humble

yourself before your God, your words were heard; and I have come because of your words" (Dan. 10:12).

From the moment you start your day devoted to God, you move God deeply, and He dispatches angels. But here are the all-important questions: Are you ready to give up a whole day? Is your heart set to understand?

You will never forget this day. Breakthroughs you have struggled to win will happen as you gaze at the Holy One.

Do you remember the truths I have tried to hammer out in this book? Every word of *Fresh Impact* has been building up to this crucial decision to sacrifice an entire day. You must become irrevocably convinced of your need to shut down your schedule.

Why does it take an entire day? Quite literally, it's because of us, not God. He isn't slow, and we most certainly do not need to stir Him to action. We are commanded in Hosea 10:12-13:

> Sow for yourselves righteousness; reap in mercy; break up your fallow ground, for it is time to seek the Lord, till He comes and rains righteousness on you...You have eaten the fruit of lies, because you trusted

in your own way, in the multitude of your mighty men.

Charles Finney wrote, "Fallow ground is ground which has once been tilled but which now lies waste. It needs to be broken up and mellowed before it is again ready to receive grain. If you want to break up the fallow ground of your heart, you must begin by looking at yourself. Examine and note the state of your mind. See where you are...Break up all the ground and turn it over. Do not balk; do not turn away because of little difficulties. Drive the plough right through them. Go deep and turn the ground up so that it will all be mellow and soft. Then it will be ready to receive the seed and bear fruit a hundredfold."[1]

This will be a day you will never forget. Breakthroughs you have struggled to win all of your life will happen within you as you gaze at the Holy One. But your flesh will rage against your decision to give up a whole day. Slay the flesh with these facts:

1. **Prayer redeems your time.** Say this to yourself: I can take the time to pray a whole day because I will not lose time; I will gain it. Prayer always more than replaces the time it uses up.

Prayer empowers you to expose thieves that steal your time, so prayer will make your life more effective. Moreover, because God's blessing will be on your actions, you will get things done more quickly.

2. **You are not being irresponsible.** You are not neglecting loved ones by taking a whole day to pray.

The people you love benefit most when you walk in the power of God. Your mate, your children and all the people you love need you to be a fresh impact. They are the immediate beneficiaries of your day of power.

3. It is your ultimate statement of faith. By slamming the brakes on your routine, you are telling the Lord that He is your God in a way that nothing else can. Not only this, but you are confessing that the unseen world is more real than the natural world (see 2 Cor. 4:18).

Now comes another urgent question. Have you received fresh fire? Being drenched by the Spirit is an utter necessity.

Fresh impact is predicated on fresh fire. Fresh impact is the exploit, the special effect, the strategic action, the heaven-sent tactic which most quickly devastates the enemy. But fresh impact must be fueled by fresh fire. Here is how I describe it in my book *Fresh Fire:* "Pentecostals presume that their initial baptism of power is a final baptism of power."[2]

When God empowered you to be a witness, that was to be the first of a series of encounters with the Holy Spirit. You need to have repeated infusions of power at key points in your life.

Corporately, the church must learn that returning to God for fresh fire is a proper reaction to crisis. There are three major crises that call for fresh fire.

1. Carnality and shallowness are rampant among believers.
2. The church has been mired in confusion and lacks direction.
3. The enemy has risen up to destroy the work of God.

The pioneers of the Pentecostal movement at the turn of the century recognized this need and called solemn assemblies based on the words of Joel:

Consecrate a fast, call a sacred assembly; gather the elders and all the inhabitants of the land into the house of the Lord your God, and cry out to the Lord (Joel 1:14).

Corporately, the church must learn that returning to God for fresh fire is a proper reaction to crisis.

Here is a guide from *Fresh Fire* on how to receive it: "Not only are you determined to seek; you want to seek correctly. To do so means to hark back to when you first received the baptism in the Holy Spirit. You came as a child, trusting the Lord's mercy and believing in His desire to baptize you. Then you waited worshipfully in His presence. Do it again; come in that attitude again."[3]

> So I say to you, ask, and it will be given to you; seek, and you will find; knock, and it will be opened to you. For everyone who asks receives, and he who seeks finds, and to him who knocks it will be opened (Luke 11:9-10).

Whether you need the original baptism of fire or a new outpouring, make this a priority on your day of power. After you have entered His courts with praise, ask for the Holy Spirit's overflow.

Finally, remember that the real victory of this day is to get there. Don't worry about what God will or will not say. Just get there!

But wait — there's something I want you to take with you on that day.

EIGHT

STEP 2:
WRITE DOWN YOUR HEART'S DESIRES

Years ago I was in the mountains near Los Angeles preaching at a youth camp. The big wooden tabernacle was full of young people. I was outside in the parking lot pacing and praying. For no apparent reason I kept glancing at a little bronze Chevy Nova Super Sport. I thought it was gorgeous! Mind you, I was not being carnal. I was praying fervently for that evening's meeting, but this car kept distracting me.

The strangest urge came over me. I had an over-powering compulsion to put my hands on that car. Next I was shocked by what came out of my mouth: "In the name of Jesus, I claim this car!" Afterward I went in and preached, and I didn't give the car another thought.

A few days later I was back in Los Angeles preaching in a home fellowship meeting. During my sermon a woman in the back of the living room began crying. Assuming it was the Lord dealing with her, I simply kept on preaching. Soon her weeping grew so loud that there was no way to ignore her.

She shouted at me, "I can't stand it anymore!" I wondered if my preaching was really that bad! Suddenly she opened her purse and threw her car keys at me. They bounced off my chest. "Take it! Take it!" she begged.

We would have no peace until I agreed to go outside and see the car she was giving me. The whole Bible study group walked out with us. I cannot describe the chill that went through me when my eyes lighted on the very car I had claimed in the mountains!

Let me add quickly that I accepted her sacrificial gift only because I knew it was God's doing. And it wasn't long before Jesus miraculously gave that woman a new car.

More thrilling than getting a new car was my great discovery of God's unique love shown by giving us the very desires of our hearts.

I wanted a car just like that one. In fact, it was precisely what I wanted, and my Father in heaven knew better than I did what would make me happy.

This miracle was so important because I had some inward insecurity, a holdover from an abusive childhood, that was crippling me as a leader. I felt that God instructed me to delight myself in His work and that as I did He would overcome in me those emotional wounds. I focused on obedience, and God focused on my need. This became one of the greatest miracles of my life.

> Delight yourself also in the Lord, and He shall give you the desires of your heart (Ps. 37:4).

Though these words are familiar to us, their real power is lost in our cynical natures. Your heart's desires are very important to Jesus. In actuality He put those desires in your heart.

So what does all this have to do with fresh impact? Surely fresh impact is something I do for God and others, and it cannot happen until I die to all my heart's desires.

That is possibly the greatest spiritual misunderstanding of all time.

God doesn't want you to abandon your heart's desires; He wants you to tell Him what they are. As a matter of fact, list them and take them with you when you ask for fresh impact.

Hear me very carefully. We have been created to seek rewards for achievement. Not only that, but seeing God as a rewarder is a prerequisite to entering His presence.

> But without faith it is impossible to please Him, for he who comes to God must believe that He is, and that He is a rewarder of those who diligently seek Him (Heb. 11:6).

Few people in history were as in touch with their heart's desires as Hannah was. She longed to be a mother, and her appeal to Jehovah was an unadulterated plea for motherhood.

But here is a strange fact: God had closed her womb!

> But to Hannah he would give a double portion, for he loved Hannah, although the Lord had closed her womb. And her rival also provoked her severely, to make her miserable, because the Lord had closed her womb (1 Sam. 1:5-6).

Why would God do such a thing? Isn't that just plain cruel? Look deeper. Her time with a closed womb intensified her heart's desire.

God creates and intensifies desires of the heart! That car, for example, was something I was made to desire in a very short time. Other, deeper longings are brought to life over longer periods of time.

Some of the greatest frustrations of your life have been orchestrated to deepen a craving in your heart. These heartfelt wishes are a very essential part of you, and they have the power to produce a cry from your soul to God. This is a mighty gift! Your cry impacts God as few things can.

> If you then, being evil, know how to give good gifts to your children, how much more will your Father who is in heaven give good things to those who ask Him! (Matt. 7:11).

Hannah's profound desire for a child endowed her with a focused prayer. Hannah did not go to pray for revival. She was not asking for a mighty move of God — she just wanted children.

Some of the greatest frustrations of your life have been orchestrated to deepen a craving in your heart.

You want joy. You want success. You want love at home and a special someone with whom to share your life. Your heavenly Father is intimately acquainted with all of your desires.

So right now get in touch with your heart and write down your heart's desires. This list must accompany you into the presence of Jesus.

You will find your miracle in a marriage of pleading for your heart's desires and making a shocking discovery about God in the process.

NINE

STEP 3:

LEND GOD YOUR DREAM

By now you should be holding a list of your heart's desires. It is time to bring them to God. You are not laying them down to be burned in an act of self-humiliation. You are asking Jesus to fulfill them.

Let me reveal to you what I believe is one of the greatest misconceptions about heroes of faith. We have this image of them as victims of the call of God.

We believe that their enjoyment of life was crushed under the truck tires of God's purpose for them.

They were holy, and, yes, they did sacrifice much and continually deny self, but they lived rich lives and obtained surprise blessings all along the way.

Even today I notice that vessels of God who are mightily used by Him share these traits: They enjoy interests outside of ministry, they love life, they laugh a lot, they are competitive, and yet they do not take themselves too seriously. These qualities do not interfere with their work. On the contrary, their celebration of life increases their focus and visionary zeal.

Here is the point I have tried to make repeatedly in this book. Because our heart longings are a big part of how God made us, He blends our fulfillment into our fresh impact. This is how the Lord evokes a total commitment, a labor of joy from His servants.

Was it selfish of David to ask,

> What shall be done for the man who kills this Philistine and takes away the reproach from Israel? For who is this uncircumcised Philistine, that he should defy the armies of the living God? (1 Sam. 17:26).

We can see David's zeal for God's honor in this verse. He wanted Goliath dead for all the right reasons, but he was also thinking about his goals and aspirations for the future.

Believe me, I have seen the other kind of spiritual leaders, those who are always somber, even morbid. They continually recite to you all that they have lost for the sake of the gospel. They describe "God's dealings" with them as if they were showing you scars. But in all their joyless labor they rarely fulfill a great vision or reach lost people.

Look again at Hannah. When she entered God's presence, she did not pray for revival in Israel. She did not come to promote the cause of righteousness. She was in fact reduced to one unending cry for motherhood. All she wanted was children.

Because our heart longings are a big part of how God made us, He blends our fulfillment into our fresh impact.

Here comes the secret of fresh impact! God was the One growing that heart cry in her. First He closed her womb, and then He allowed her rival to harass her: "And her rival also provoked her severely, to make her miserable, because the Lord had closed her womb" (1 Sam. 1:6). She could not eat but only wept until finally she collapsed at the door of the tabernacle. Eli, the priest, assumed she was drunk, because now her cry transcended words — it was total heart language.

Hannah explained, "No, my lord, I am a woman of sorrowful spirit. I have drunk neither wine nor intoxicating drink, but have poured out my soul before the Lord" (v. 15). There it is! She poured out her soul to the Lord, and like a bucket of water poured into a pump to prime it, so it was that God began pouring out His soul to Hannah.

This is the timeless discovery of spiritual giants since the garden: "Deep calls unto deep at the noise of Your waterfalls" (Ps. 42:7). Her deep cry touched the depth of God.

Our profound longings bring us into a position in which God and His child can create a miracle. It is as though our overwhelming grief tunes our spirits to the frequency of God's grief.

God had no prophet in Israel; Hannah found empathy with God. He had no prophet; she had no son. Their mutual yearnings, which by the rules of math add up to double zero, instead resulted in double provision.

> Then she made a vow and said, "O Lord of hosts, if You will indeed look on the affliction of Your maidservant and remember me, and not forget Your maidservant, but will give Your maidservant a male child, then I will give him to the Lord all the days of his life, and no razor shall come upon his head (1 Sam. 1:11).

This is nothing short of a model fresh-impact prayer!

In the process of asking for your heart's desires you discover the grief God bears. But not just any grief; it is that sorrow which you are uniquely equipped to heal — your fresh impact!

The Bible says in Isaiah 53:3 that Jesus was a "Man of sorrows and acquainted with grief." Paul referred to the "fellowship of His sufferings" in Philippians 3:10. Though we cannot heal God's grief, we can, by sensing His grief, be violently changed as Isaiah wrote, "Woe is me, for I am undone! Because I am a man of unclean lips, and I dwell in the midst of a people of unclean lips; for my eyes have seen the King, the Lord of hosts" (Is. 6:5).

After that, God called Isaiah to serve him, saying: "Whom shall I send, and who will go for Us?"

Isaiah responded: "Here am I! Send me."

You are going to hear from God, and in that moment you will cease to ask for your heart's desires any longer. You will lend them to the Lord.

Because of Hannah, the prophet Samuel was born.

> And the Lord visited Hannah, so that she conceived and bore three sons and two daughters. Meanwhile the child Samuel grew before the Lord (1 Sam. 2:21).

What are you waiting for? Pour out your soul to God. The marriage of your heart to God's heart will create the miracle. And you will discover what your personally designed fresh impact is.

TEN

STEP 4:
I AM TO...

A fresh impact can be written in a few words. For David those words were "I am to kill this giant and remove this reproach from Israel." For Esther they were "I will go to the king and save my people." Moses' fresh impact statement was "I am to go to Egypt and set the children of Israel free." Joshua's revealed impact followed Moses': "I am to take the people into the promised land."

All Bible heroes received simple orders at the point of their calling, and these words became core beliefs that launched a lifetime of effectiveness.

Look at Saul of Tarsus. Jesus said to him in Acts 9:6, "You will be told what you must do." That promise is yours, my friend. *You will be told.*

Once His words resonate through you, they will alter your self-concept. God's voice will preempt the facts of your life. This is your defining moment, your manifesto.

Preconceived limits won't matter anymore. You will be able to complete this all-important mission statement: "I am to...."

You will do as Habakkuk 2:2 says,

> Then the Lord answered me and said: "Write the vision and make it plain on tablets. That he may run who reads it."

There will come words right from the depth of God. They will cause you and those around you to run with a vision.

These verses reveal how to hear your fresh impact:

> The Lord God has given Me the tongue of the learned, that I should know how to speak a word in season to him who is weary. He awakens Me morning by morning, He awakens My ear to hear as the

learned. The Lord God has opened My ear; and I was not rebellious, nor did I turn away (Is. 50:4-5).

In this day devoted to God, you will hear from God; then your heart will change, and you will know what to do.

The awakened ear. Listening is one of the greatest gifts, and hearing from God is the highest form of listening. No one ever learned anything while talking. Likewise, in prayer there comes the time of silence when the Holy Spirit awakens your ear.

All Bible heroes received simple orders which became core beliefs that launched a lifetime of effectiveness.

Hannah showed us how to get the attention of Jehovah. She cried from her heart, and it went straight to God's heart. This triggers the voice of the Lord.

How will you know when He speaks? First there is the promise that we, His sheep, know His voice (John 10:4). But you will also have a signal that He is about to speak. In the midst of your deep crying will come an indescribable sense that you have been heard, and a sigh of relief will rise from your soul. This is followed by a holy awe that quells fear and silences your heart. Then you will find within yourself a sensitivity, an awakened ear. You are now listening from your heart.

Your circle of love. It is very possible that your first message from Jesus will not be words but an urgency you feel. You are starting to care about something beyond your own life. You are being influenced by the yearnings of God. He is depositing in you His grief and His love so you can respond to a specific need.

Even though your fresh impact can only happen through God, it is tailored to fit you.

This is what Pastor Tommy Barnett of Phoenix First Assembly of God in Phoenix, Arizona, calls your circle of love. You may suddenly feel your heart going out to children from a specific neighborhood, the elderly or perhaps youth gangs, AIDS victims, bikers or even politicians. The list is endless. This circle of love is the location of your fresh impact.

David Wilkerson told me once, "The will of God grows on you." Gentle impressions become waves of stronger urgency until you have a clear conviction.

Here is your empathy with God. You lend Him your heart's desires so that He can have the available life He has needed. Again look at Matthew 6:32-33: "For the pagans run after all these things, and your heavenly Father knows that you need them. But seek first his kingdom and his righteousness, and all these things will be given to you as well" (NIV).

God is not against our having what the "pagans run after." But He wants us to run after the issues of the kingdom *first*, and He will add to that our hearts' desires.

One way you will know it is God moving in your heart is if your concern is over a need you have passed by every day and never before noticed. How many times did Peter pass the crippled man before that miracle day at the temple gate called Beautiful (see Acts 3:1-8)?

What you hear from the Holy Spirit goes to the heart first and then to the mind. After you have found your circle of love, your mind is ready for a plan. But first you need to write down your target for fresh impact.

"Lord, what do You want me to do?" This simple prayer leads to your written fresh impact.

Once Gideon understood it was the Midianites whom he had to attack, he pleaded with God for details.

The exploit you are about to commence for the glory of God will be within the context of your personality, though it will be beyond your natural talent. Even though your fresh impact can only happen through God, it is tailored to fit you so that it launches from your natural talents into supernatural effectiveness. The Lord begins with what you have.

The plan is coming. Jesus means to reveal it to

you either by a flash of clear direction or a gradually focusing strategy. Do not hesitate to write down a rough picture of what you are sensing. You can always refine it later. Start writing! "I am to...."

This is your personal commission from the throne of God. You will cease to struggle; you will walk in confidence because you are not creating a plan — you are obeying a plan.

Imagine our nation full of Spirit-led believers of impact. No more hit-and-miss projects but an army engaged in the purest form of effectiveness!

Now that you are writing down your fresh impact, you are ready for what comes next — the power by which God makes you equal to your mission. I call it being *rendered effective.*

ELEVEN

STEP 5:
RENDERED EFFECTIVE

Is there a nagging doubt in you about your fresh impact? Is there a big question? You may be wondering, How can I do what God reveals to me to do? Even if I am told what I am supposed to do, how do I know I can do it?

Let the story of Saul in 1 Samuel 9 teach us:

There was a man of Benjamin whose name

was Kish the son of Abiel, the son of Zeror, the son of Bechorath, the son of Aphiah, a Benjamite, a mighty man of power. And he had a choice and handsome son whose name was Saul. There was not a more handsome person than he among the children of Israel. From his shoulders upward he was taller than any of the people.

Now the donkeys of Kish, Saul's father, were lost. And Kish said to his son Saul, "Please take one of the servants with you, and arise, go and look for the donkeys."

So he passed through the mountains of Ephraim and through the land of Shalisha, but they did not find them. Then they passed through the land of Shaalim, and they were not there. Then he passed through the land of the Benjamites, but they did not find them.

When they had come to the land of Zuph, Saul said to his servant who was with him, "Come let us return, lest my father cease caring about the donkeys and become worried about us." And he said to him, "Look now, there is in this city a man of God, and he is an honorable man; all that he says surely comes to pass. So let us go there; perhaps he can show us the way that we should go."

Then Saul said to his servant, "But look, if we go, what shall we bring the man? For the bread in our vessels is all gone, and there is no present to bring to the man of God. What do we have?"

And the servant answered Saul again and said, "Look, I have here at hand one-fourth of a shekel of silver. I will give that to the man of God, to tell us our way" (vv. 1-8).

The most that the young, scared Saul could have expected from his encounter with the prophet was guidance to find lost animals. Instead he was in for the most unexpected shock of his life. God had prepared Samuel to meet Saul. The prophet was told what Saul's life impact would be.

Dunamis *starts with an explosion of boldness and confidence, but it goes on to instill in you gifts to carry out a task.*

Now the Lord had told Samuel in his ear the day before Saul came, saying, "Tomorrow about this time I will send you a man from the land of Benjamin, and you shall anoint him commander over My people Israel, that he may save My people from the hand of the Philistines; for I have

> looked upon My people, because their cry
> has come to Me."
>
> So when Samuel saw Saul, the Lord
> said to him, "There he is, the man of
> whom I spoke to you. This one shall reign
> over My people" (1 Sam. 9:15-17).

Saul's reaction is classic.

> And Saul answered and said, "Am I not a
> Benjamite, of the smallest of the tribes of
> Israel, and my family the least of all the
> families of the tribe of Benjamin? Why
> then do you speak like this to me?" (v. 21).

Now you and I have been over all this before
with Gideon. Your reaction to God's call can be to
dismiss it as nonsense because you see your weaknesses and inabilities.

Step 5 of fresh impact is summed up in Samuel's
solemn promise and command to Saul, and it is our
charge as well. Samuel is anointing Saul king and
saying:

> Then the Spirit of the Lord will come
> upon you, and you will prophesy with
> them and be turned into another man.
> And let it be, when these signs come to
> you, that you do as the occasion demands;
> for God is with you (10:6-7).

What Samuel described here is the wondrous process by which a common human is altered and empowered to fulfill a mission from God.

The Greek word *dunamis* is often interpreted as "explosive power," but it is far, far more. It is best described as "the power of God that renders you effective." *Dunamis* starts with an explosion of boldness and confidence, but it goes on to instill in you gifts to carry out a task. Ultimately it puts the will to endure in the mind of the vessel.

There are three features of *dunamis* which render you effective. These facets are seen in verses 6 and 7 in the promise from Samuel to Saul.

1. Explosion: "The Spirit of the Lord will come upon you." You will "be turned into another man."

2. Gifts: "...when these signs come to you."

3. The will to endure: "Do as the occasion demands."

Let's look a little closer at each one.

1. An explosion of confidence, boldness and certainty about your mission.

But you shall receive power [*dunamis*] when the Holy Spirit has come upon you; and you shall be witnesses to Me in Jerusalem, and in all Judea and Samaria, and to the end of the earth (Acts 1:8).

The clear purpose of this explosion is to throw

you out of your routine and launch you into a radical new direction. This immersion of fire gives your system the shock necessary to jump-start action. Natural fear and human reluctance vanish as a strong current rushes you to your destined impact.

Whether you need the baptism in the Holy Spirit or a fresh-fire enduement, this explosion is a universal prerequisite to beginning an undertaking for God.

2. Imparted skills.

> Having then gifts differing according to the grace that is given to us, let us use them: if prophecy, let us prophesy in proportion to our faith; or ministry, let us use it in our ministering; he who teaches, in teaching; he who exhorts, in exhortation; he who gives, with liberality; he who leads, with diligence, he who shows mercy, with cheerfulness (Rom. 12:6-8).
>
> And I thank Christ Jesus our Lord who has enabled me, because He counted me faithful, putting me into the ministry (1 Tim. 1:12).

There is an incontrovertible fact of the Bible: All who receive power receive gifts. The empowered become the enabled.

One thing that moved me to write *Fresh Impact* was

the darkness in the church right now. We have suffered through a time of vain human talent and counterfeit gifts of God. The toll has been incalculable.

It is time for the church to discover that God imparts to millions of common Christians the power and gifts needed for impact. It is time for mass effectiveness.

As I said before, when I look for a new staff member I do not seek talent first; I seek a loyal heart. Talent can be added to a proven vessel, but it is hard to add loyalty to talent.

As you head to the front line, new gifts will surface that fit your impact statement perfectly.

A therapist once asked a juvenile delinquent a question: "If a lion jumped through that window right at you, what would you do?"

The youth's answer was instant: "I'd raise my rifle and shoot!"

The baffled therapist asked, "Where did you get the rifle?"

The young man retorted, "Where did you get the lion?"

We will receive the gifts necessary to shoot down whatever jumps at us!

> *The purpose of this explosion is to throw you out of your routine and launch you into a radical new direction.*

> If you then, being evil, know how to give
> good gifts to your children, how much more
> will your Father who is in heaven give good
> things to those who ask Him! (Matt. 7:11).

3. The will to sustain impact and renew impact.

> Therefore I remind you to stir up the gift
> of God which is in you through the laying
> on of my hands. For God has not given us
> a spirit of fear, but of power and of love
> and of a sound mind (2 Tim. 1:6-7).

All of *dunamis* is a gift, and endurance is no less! The great awakeners of history were not just miracles of power and talent; they were miracles of tenacity. Paul explains his gift of perseverance.

> But by the grace of God I am what I am,
> and His grace toward me was not in vain;
> but I labored more abundantly than they
> all, yet not I, but the grace of God which
> was with me (1 Cor. 15:10).

To stay effective you must build on your God-imparted gifts, sharpen your use of them and connect with others who are already effective. Within you is a dynamo that refuses to stop until the race is finished.

In the face of any and every setback, this radiating gift of "stick-to-itiveness" will replenish and carry you. Your heart will say, No matter what, I'm going on! This will to endure is actually the love of God that "endures all things" (1 Cor. 13:7).

Love is the fuel to use gifts correctly. First Corinthians 12:31 says, "But earnestly desire the best gifts. And yet I show you a more excellent way." Paul was referring here to *love.*

This grace to endure will also help you discern when embers need to be fanned into flame. If necessary, you will be willing to repeat all five steps to impact whenever it is required!

Remember that *dunamis* is:

1. The *thrill* to act (explosion).
2. The *skill* to act (gifts).
3. The *will* to sustain action (endurance).

Let God render you effective. No verse more clearly shows the three facets of *dunamis* or the promise of mass impact than the following.

> Those who do wickedly against the covenant he shall corrupt with flattery; but the people who know their God shall be strong, and carry out great exploits (Dan. 11:32).

FIRST THE CHURCH, THEN THE WORLD

TWELVE

A PLEA FOR IMPACT PASTORS AND CHURCHES

I f you are a pastor, if you love a pastor or if you have a heart for your church, this word is for you. I know too well the pressure a modern preacher works under.

Today's clergyman faces a vocal, critical genera-tion of Christians. Monstrous accusations can come out of nowhere and show no mercy, even to the minister's wife and children. The news media enlarge the problem by portraying all men of the cloth as crooks. Governmental tax agencies target churches, and local authorities write laws that seem blatantly designed to stop church growth. Today's preacher literally gets it from all directions.

The tragic fact is that the church helps the world to make ministry a thankless job that seems suitable only for those who want to take abuse. This is why good men get driven out of pulpits and jaded hirelings end up occupying them instead.

Amazingly, amid all this adversity, most pastors remain devoted, hard-working, sincere men of God.

While understanding all the garbage thrown at ministers, can't we still ask for exciting Sunday mornings? Or sermons that combine relevance and power? Is it irrational for me to want preachers who refuse to coddle self-absorbed baby boomers? Where are the heroes who will eject the saints out of lifestyle addiction and into fire-bred exploits from God? What will change a cheesy church into a vital force?

Before I tell you, let me mention one last lethal poison fed to pastors: church-growth advice. Some seminars are good, but many are beyond a waste of time. A mountain of useless technology and methodology is foisted on preachers desperate for growth. Time and again seductive advice has distracted pastors from prayer, where the real solution was waiting for them.

Some leaders chase growth like the cartoon coyote chases the roadrunner. So many of the exotic traps we lay end up exploding in our faces.

I have been in many church offices where slick binders and videos line the bookshelves. They guarantee to gather people, but they end up only gathering dust. What really irks me is "experts." While they tout these surefire "growth factors," they inadvertently dismiss smaller works as having no potential.

A fresh-impact church is a power-and-gifts warehouse — and a weapon.

Once, two stunt men in Hollywood decided they wanted to be movie stars, so they went to a casting director. After their screen tests the director sat them down. To the first he said, "You can't act." To the other he said, "Sorry, but your Adam's apple is too big. Both of you should forget about movies."

The two left dejected. One asked the other, "What are you going to do now?" The response was, "I am going to take acting lessons, but I don't know what you can do about your Adam's apple!"

Who were these two men? Burt Reynolds and Clint Eastwood.[1] (No word on what the casting director is doing now). Likewise, if a "growth expert" says you don't have what it takes, I say, "Bunk!"

It is time to stop this madness and build an impact church! What do I mean by this? A fresh-impact church is a power-and-gifts warehouse —

and a weapon. It is a center of manifold effectiveness. In an impact church the pastor has written down the strategic destiny of his congregation as he has heard it from the Holy Spirit. He has embedded this living word in their hearts and ignited action. The stated impact becomes the battle cry.

Let us not belabor the reasons why we need fresh impact. The alternatives are way too obvious — and tragic: churches that have the Word but no moving of the Holy Spirit; churches that are all emotion but are sadly lacking in any biblical foundation.

Many churches run a strength into the ground to cover a weakness. Still others bounce from crisis to crisis applying stopgap measures that create a congregation with multiple personalities.

Because stopgap measures are not from God, they won't last. You as a leader will find yourself adding more and more half cures and quick fixes. Every time you change direction you will leave some people trapped in the previous emphasis you were using. Soon you will have pockets of different teachings and loyalties among the people, hence a church with multiple personalities.

You as the leader must be willing to stop everything!

"But, Mario," you say, "if I stop, it will get worse!" Well, maybe things are worse than you thought. So bad, in fact, that stopping can't make it any worse! You are likely in the position of having nothing to lose and everything to gain.

Stop the madness! Do these things to birth a fresh impact in your church:

1. Get fire and impact yourself.

Just because you are a vessel of God does not mean there is fresh fire in you. Your private day of hearing from God is truly essential. The five steps to a written impact (section 2 of this book) are for you too! But on this day devoted to God you should seek the objective of your church — the mass impact for your people.

2. Prepare the written impact statement so that those who read it can run with it.

Try to remember all that I have said about the urgency of objective. An army that doesn't know its objective is fooled into wars of attrition.

Church as usual may be killing you gently with results that seem good but merely hide their drain on your resources. They are distracting you from your true destiny.

Read your fresh-impact statement to the congregation. God will anoint it. It will unleash the people's gifts, and they will run with it!

3. Call for a congregational day of power.

Do not worry if only a handful come; these people represent your prophetic core. These are the ones who will stick with you. Never underestimate their potential.

Just a few hundred came out to David while he hid in the cave.

And everyone who was in distress, everyone who was in debt, and everyone who was discontented gathered to him. So he became captain over them. And there were about four hundred men with him (1 Sam. 22:2).

From every angle this ragtag group looked anything but promising. But under David's leadership they became, man for man, the most potent fighting team in history.

God starts with a willing core, but too many pastors hold on blindly to people who will never serve but endlessly demand to be served. Remove the wet logs by calling for a day of power! Let the real fuel in your church flame up.

There are three things you should give your congregation in this day of power:

1. A clearly written fresh-impact declaration.

It should be complete but not exhaustive. Make it thorough enough to satisfy the visionary appetite of the people. Your church too will have this supernatural baptism of unity and willingness.

2. A concise phrase that epitomizes your fresh-impact declaration.

This hook phrase will be both a war cry and a reinforcement of the objective. For example, the mission manifesto of Mario Murillo Ministries declares our commitment to a worldwide impact with piercing preaching that targets secular evil with signs and wonders. We invade Satan's strongholds with a message from God, and we do it without apology.

> For I am not ashamed of the gospel of Christ, for it is the power of God to salvation for everyone who believes, for the Jew first and also for the Greek (Rom. 1:16).

Everyone on my staff knows it all boils down to this phrase: the power of God to everyone!

3. The opportunity to stand and formally embrace God's call to this impact.

The covenant you are making will release power to fulfill it. Look at what happened when Hezekiah proclaimed Judah's fresh impact.

> Also the hand of God was on Judah to give them singleness of heart to obey the command of the king and the leaders, at the word of the Lord (2 Chron. 30:12).

Much power has been squandered in our insistence that the pastor be the veritable witness of the church to the community. He should instead be the leader of the impact. His chief function must be to release the whole impact in a concert of effectiveness.

This means that he brings the latent gifts of the body to the surface. He releases many voices, looses a myriad of power gifts and validates fresh methods. Then he blends all of this until the manifold response of God to present oppression and evil is felt by his city.

The ultimate pastor leads the sheep into fresh fire and into the discovery of their destiny in the local miracle. Then the church will be an impact witness on society. And he welcomes fresh impact miracles.

THIRTEEN

A PLEA FOR
FRESH-IMPACT MIRACLES

You and I have both been in meetings where we felt squeamish. We knew inside that what was being purported to be a "move of God" was nothing but an emotional binge. Sensationalism has plagued Spirit-filled Christians since the time of the book of Acts. Paul tried to inject sanity into the Corinthian chaos. They abused the gift of tongues and threatened the whole movement's credibility.

It seems that from God's perspective few things can be worse than miracle abuse. It is sobering to realize that you can take a divine gift and pervert its intention.

You cannot appreciate the enormity of this tragedy unless you first see the original glory and the impact potential of the gifts of the Holy Spirit.

> But to each one of us grace was given according to the measure of Christ's gift. Therefore He says: *"When He ascended on high, He led captivity captive, and gave gifts to men."* (Now this, *"he ascended"* — what does it mean but that He also first descended into the lower parts of the earth? He who descended is also the One who ascended far above all the heavens, that He might fill all things.)
>
> And He himself gave some to be apostles, some prophets, some evangelists, and some pastors and teachers, for the equipping of the saints for the work of ministry, for the edifying of the body of Christ, till we all come to the unity of the faith and of the knowledge of the Son of God, to a perfect man, to the measure of the stature of the fullness of Christ; that we should no longer be children, tossed to and fro and carried about with every wind of doctrine, by the trickery of men, in the cunning

craftiness of deceitful plotting, but, speaking the truth in love, may grow up in all things into Him who is the head — Christ (Eph. 4:7-15).

Here we see the awesomeness of the power gifts to make giants out of mere Christians. Paul felt keenly the need for sound expression of gifts and miracles and committed three entire chapters to instruction on them: 1 Corinthians 12, 13 and 14.

He started by telling the Corinthians that he did not want them to be ignorant. The apostle put it very strongly in 2 Corinthians 10:4: "For the weapons of our warfare are not carnal but mighty in God for pulling down strongholds."

Do you see the power of what you just read? I believe that these power gifts are the weapons of our warfare, and weapons are the most important element of war next to the soldier himself. There is a passion I hold: it is that the work of the church, the edification of believers and the task of piercing evil are futile without the correct use of miracles.

The gifts of God are not carnal. They are not based on the sensual or the emotional, but they are mighty. Our handicap is that we cannot imagine the mighty without the emotional. Many preachers function from a stance of disbelief in the might of God inherent to the gifts of the Spirit.

Why else would you whip a crowd? Why else would you "induce" unless you felt that the force you were working with needed inducement? And when the atmosphere of a meeting is carnal, it can only appeal to the baser saints seeking a buzz. But to outsiders it is just so much madness.

This is Paul's point exactly in 1 Corinthians 14:23. It is bad enough that we are considered loony by outsiders; it is worse when you realize that some of us actually revel in it.

But not only are these gifts mighty; they are mighty with purpose — to the tearing down of strongholds.

Have you noticed that the news media complain about healing evangelists but rarely about healing?

The gifts of the Holy Spirit have a target. They are going after those places that are strongly held by evil. This means that the true and ultimate demonstration of power is outside the church walls. It is also outside the entertainment needs of bored believers.

Here we are forcing the mighty gifts of God to conform to lesser purposes!

The sooner we see this disastrous deception, the sooner we will stop interfering and start seeing the impact the power gifts were meant to have — dismantling demonic beachheads that bind masses of beloved souls.

Paul has another shocker for us. He uses the

word *if* in two strategic places in 1 Corinthians 14:23-25:

> Therefore if the whole church comes together in one place, and all speak with tongues, and there come in those who are uninformed or unbelievers, will they not say that you are out of your mind? But if all prophesy, and an unbeliever or an uninformed person comes in, he is convinced by all, he is convicted by all. And thus the secrets of his heart are revealed; and so, falling down on his face, he will worship God and report that God is truly among you.

Two phrases jump out at me: "Therefore if" and "But if." Under the circumstances of the first "if," Paul said unbelievers would react this way: "Will they not say that you are out of your mind?" But under the conditions of the second "if," Paul said the unbeliever, "falling down on his face," would "worship God and report that God is truly among you."

Here is a chilling example of the power of choice that is at the heart of this book. Do we want our nation to dismiss us as buffoons, or do we want a nation to fall before God and declare that God is truly among us?

There is a choice! There is a fresh-impact choice. If there is even a remote possibility that this is right, then I believe an urgent call must be put out to all leaders. Emotional rallies that ignore the Holy Spirit's objectives are much more criminal than we previously thought.

Can you see how frightened Satan is that the secret of fresh-impact miracles might be widely known? Remember the chapter titled "We Are Not Supposed to Leave Quietly"? This is where I first referred to us as stewards over miracles.

The earthquake in Philippi was God's doing, but it was up to Paul to enforce the objective of the earthquake. Paul forced the city fathers to submit to the work of God. The apostle did his part to use the weapon on the stronghold.

Here is my plea: Let us clean up our part in the miracle process!

It is God's part to heal, to demonstrate power and to deliver, but it is our role to hear with spiritual ears what the Holy Ghost wants. It is up to us to verify the meaning and intention of the supernatural act.

Have you noticed that the news media complain about healing evangelists but rarely about healing? The miracle is not the problem; it is our fleshly trappings they reject. Their contention is with "charismania" and "Pentecostal paraphernalia."

Just as clearly as we can choose to be irrelevant, immature and selfish, we can choose fresh-impact miracles!

Here are three urgent prerequisites to fresh-impact miracles:

1. Purify your motive for wanting miracles.

Some painful questions must be asked here. Do you condone entertainment to draw people? Are you after people's money? Do you borrow on other people's crowd-drawing hype methods? Do you want a large church more than a large impact?

We need a jolt! We need to remember that Jesus loves our communities infinitely more than we do. He wants to heal and deliver even more than we want these miracles.

We do not need to persuade God to work; we need to stop interfering. Cleansing ourselves of hype allows a new picture to merge — that of an aggressive God whose passion is mass miracles. God is on a mission to your area. Our impact is the inevitable result of lining up with God's work.

2. Verify the miracles.

It is for God to work miracles, but it is for us to facilitate them.

Miracle abuse has polarized us so that we either tolerate everything or prohibit everything. It is not right to assume that all miracles are innocent till proven guilty or that they are all guilty till proven innocent. The key is to expect an aggressive God to do something that we are prepared for!

But when it is not of God, we stop it. We are to have neither a free-for-all nor a dead, cold meeting. We release the power but dump the sensational.

To verify miracles means that we encourage people to get medical reports to confirm miracles. To verify miracles means that we are "mainstreaming." We should stand in the middle of secular society and boldly define for the outsider what God has done.

> Now when they saw the boldness of Peter and John, and perceived that they were uneducated and untrained men, they marveled. And they realized that they had been with Jesus. And seeing the man who had been healed standing with them, they could say nothing against it (Acts 4:13-14).

We are the custodians who watch for the inevitable power gifts and escort them to their targets — while at the same time policing counterfeit gifts.

3. Make the impact choices.

- Choose to see people fall and declare God rather than see them scurry away questioning our sanity.
- Earnestly desire the best gifts. Don't stop at wanting power, but sense which gifts the Spirit of God says are best suited for your local darkness.
- Take it to the target! Resolve to do this. The targets of the Holy Spirit are outside the church walls and outside our concepts of ministry. The power of God that we seek will only intensify if we go with it to the strongholds.

If in fact it is our conviction that the miracles of the book of Acts are for today, then it is crucial for us to surrender to God to permit their proper operation.

But there is a greater crisis than this. No matter how you cut it, our nation is now supernaturally evil, and only the God-sent supernatural will prevail against this evil.

The Spirit-filled promise is that mighty gifts will tear down strongholds. Philip saw it happen:

> Then Philip went down to the city of Samaria and preached Christ to them. And the multitudes with one accord heeded the things spoken by Philip, hearing and seeing the miracles which he did. For unclean spirits, crying with a loud voice, came out of many who were possessed; and many who were paralyzed and lame were healed. And there was great joy in that city (Acts 8:5-8).

Here was a sorcerer's city swallowed up by fresh-impact miracles!

For us to continue in deliberate emotion, immaturity or denial is an inestimable sin. We are like those who would employ a cruise missile to clear weeds or to use a cure for AIDS as pimple medicine.

I believe that an era of effective submission to the power gifts awaits us — an era free of carnality and hype. Let us trade in the fickle faucet of human attempts for the healing, cleansing, resurrecting, raging river of God!

Now let's look at an example of how fresh impact in the church will change the world.

FOURTEEN

FRESH-IMPACT EXAMPLE: THE LAZARUS GENERATION

It surprised me that the most popular part of my previous book, *Fresh Fire,* was "The Lazarus Generation." This prophetic promise that God would raise up our lost youth really hit people.

Here is how I described it.

> The United States is home to a wretched generation of violent orphans.

These orphans start out as children subjected to a lethal mixture of shattered families, a cynical culture, and a ready access to guns. Television violence is their only lasting parent.

The jaded, grinding, hollow look in their eyes is a testament of national shame.

Has Satan ever brutalized a generation more? This is why I cry for them. As I cried one night, God spoke a phrase to me that would alter my whole life. "The Lazarus Generation," God said. "They're coming," God promises. "Who are they?" I wondered....

To help me, the Spirit led me to Ezekiel 37. Ezekiel had been whisked away to a bluff overlooking a valley of dry bones....

The Lord issued [to Ezekiel] an amazing command: "Prophesy to these bones that they may live."...When Ezekiel *obeyed* and prophesied, a fierce rattling began. Muscle, sinew, and skin formed out of nowhere. Suddenly there stood an exceedingly powerful army.

"*Prophesy!*" God commanded. Go from the comfortable churches to these hellholes. Prophesy to the crack addict, the teenage prostitute, the young satanists and gang leaders. Prophesy to them *that they may live!*

God will mine treasures out of darkness and out of their graves they will rise to lead the most stunning return to right-eousness America has ever seen![1]

Since I wrote this I have seen those words become reality. Fresh impact has begun to hit the Lazarus Generation.

The hellholes of our nation are opening up, and out of every kind of grave youth are being resur-rected. A new breed of young believer is being unleashed on an unwary world.

I know who they are. I've met them. They are fearless because they have already tasted death. They are abandoned to God, knowing they are living on borrowed time. Their infectious faith will touch millions. It is going to be a delight to watch the sec-ular media baffled and powerless before these youth who shatter every Christian stereotype.

Think about it. Wasn't Lazarus himself the quin-tessential fresh impact?

> Now a great many of the Jews knew that He was there; and they came, not for Jesus' sake only, but that they might also see Lazarus, whom He had raised from the dead. But the chief priests plotted to put Lazarus to death also, because on account of him many of the Jews went away and believed in Jesus (John 12:9-11).

132

They wanted to kill Lazarus. He hadn't done anything; he didn't need to. His very existence was enough to send evil running and prove that Jesus was the Christ. His sheer presence was an impact.

Go figure. They wanted to kill a man who had already been raised from the dead once! Great religious and political minds think alike.

Because the forces of darkness had no retort to this resurrected being, Lazarus could devastate them wherever he went. This is the same effect we can expect from the Lazarus Generation. No weapon formed against them will prosper!

Jesus will raise up these youth to help us. The Holy Spirit knows something we don't: Youth are the key to our own future. Without a mass youth impact our society is sunk.

Does it surprise you that youth bear the brunt of our nation's mistakes? They are a choice target of Satan for three very important reasons:

It will be a delight to watch the secular media baffled and powerless before these youth who shatter every Christian stereotype.

1) They are always the force behind cultural change; 2) they are impressionable; and 3) they are the future.

Youth are the laboratory rats that the devil utilizes to test new forms of deception.

The Lazarus impact will be radical youth reaching radical youth. You will see a massive pride of lions roaring righteousness in our land. Because of their shocking appearance and the fact that they will be former drug addicts, hookers, homosexuals, bikers, gang warlords and killers, both the world and the church will be scared of them.

The disciples were scared as the order came from Jesus to unwrap the once-dead Lazarus. "Loose him, and let him go" (John 11:44). We will hear that command again.

We can't be put off by the extreme appearance of these former dead youth. I repeat: The Lazarus Generation will be raised up too fast to change clothes. Their grave garb will be worn in the church, and we can't be the fashion police. They must meet excitement and love in our churches, not a dress code.

The Lazarus impact will result in the most amazing youth awakening our nation has ever seen. We will either embrace it and be indescribably blessed, or it will run over us like a locomotive.

To embrace the Lazarus impact we must do these things:

1. Devote all of our empty church seats to unwanted youth.

> Then he said to his servants, "The wedding is ready, but those who were invited were not worthy. Therefore go into the highways, and as many as you find, invite

to the wedding." So those servants went out into the highways and gathered together all whom they found, both bad and good. And the wedding hall was filled with guests (Matt. 22:8-10).

Face it: Most of the people we invited weren't worthy. Let's quit trying for the "right" crowd and deliberately go after the wrong crowd. Jesus never said to the world, "Go into all the churches and hear the gospel." We must die to pleasing church donors who complain about how loud the music is. Let's listen to our on-fire youth pastors. Let's open up to the Holy Spirit's seemingly strange and radical strategies for overrunning our sanctuary with youth!

The Lazarus Generation will be raised up too fast to change clothes. Their grave garb will be worn in the church.

Why not? The seats are empty anyway. Hang a sign on your heart that reads, "Lazarus Generation welcome here."

Do we know the principal of the high school? Do we know local hangouts? Do we know the gang leaders? Do we know the youth in our church who are on fire for God? Use these resources.

"But, Mario, youth can't give money."

Listen to how evil that sounds. God is rolling up

135

His sleeves to open graves of dead youth, and we are worried about money!

Go and get them. God will finance the mission. Change your church without compromising the truth of the gospel; but make changes that will draw the youth.

2. Prophesy: Lazarus, come forth!

How do you talk to a dead person? How do you call the Lazarus Generation?

Go to the tombs. These youth are not hard to find; thousands of them in the gangs of Los Angeles are expected to die before their twentieth birthday. Look in Detroit, where an eleven-year-old boy was executed by gangs because he was a murderer himself and had committed over a hundred felonies in three months.

Try San Francisco, where an Eagle Scout from a good family brought a loaded Uzi gun to class. They are in our middle schools, where some polls show that Satan is their chief father figure. Or look in New York, where mothers put bullet-proof vests on their five-year-olds when they go to school. Check in any major city where thousands of children are homeless or trapped in prostitution.

We are in a nationwide disaster of our youth that is so extensive that you and I cannot go anywhere without seeing the spirit of death on our youth.

Call them what Jesus calls them. Jesus shouted, "Lazarus!" Our shout must be equally specific. We are not to call them junkies, gays, hookers or criminals. They are the beloved, destined for resurrection.

136

They are kidnapped royalty. Our preaching must be saturated with that revelation.

We are not to add to the weight of their sin with our words. We are to seize them with the thrill of their own destiny.

Let our nation's pulpits be purified of attacks on their appearance and behavior. Let us ignore their costumes and call them by the names that cause resurrection: "accepted in the beloved," "a royal priesthood," "chosen generation."

Command them to come forth. Here is at once a prophecy and a command. Jesus was not suggesting resurrection to Lazarus. He was commanding it.

We have an orphaned generation. Family ties are dead — no father, no structure, no order and no limits.

It always amazes me how extreme youth reactions are. If I put down their music, clothes and actions, they instantly check out. But if I thunder like an angry but loving father who commands them to stop dying and scolds them for refusing to embrace the life they were born to live, they break and invade the kingdom en masse.

"Come forth" are two words oozing with power, direction and meaning. These are all-encompassing words. They mean, "Hey, you! Yeah, you in that tomb. Get out now! Walk straight ahead, drop your death and come into the life!"

Shame on you preachers who have no time to discern the Lazarus Generation! They do not respect murky speeches or psycho-babble. They want absolutes. They want integrity. They want clear direction. "Come forth" requires no lip reading.

3. **Loose them and let them go.** Just as Jesus told the people to unwrap Lazarus, so we must obey. The Lazarus Generation must clean up, drop drugs, stop sexual sin and renounce the works of darkness.

But we must not rewrap them in church grave clothes. We must not let the Christian Clone Factory get their hands on them and try to make them short-haired, card-carrying Republicans. We must not dull the edge of their uniqueness. We must give them the Word and the Spirit, but not sterile styles.

Eli told Samuel to listen to God's voice. Letting them go means we let them listen; we let them receive strategies; we help them discern visions. Ideas from God will boil up in their spirits, and we are not to squelch, but to channel, their newfound energy.

The Lazarus Generation knows the language of the lost, and we can contribute the good news.

Before pride and jealousy destroy us we must remember how urgently we need the Lazarus Generation and how desperate our situation is.

Our nation cannot hear us! The church is dismissed as a collection of escapists and relics. We are rearranging deck chairs on a sinking ocean liner.

But the Lazarus Generation knows the language

of the lost, and we can contribute the good news. Our resurrected youth are connected to the lost souls from which we are now isolated. They will reintroduce us to our mission field and be our interpreters. They are the fuse to our national impact.

Try to picture this:

- Small pockets of fire breaking out here and there.
- Humble hearts receiving *dunamis.*
- People abandoning their fears and calling for days of power in which leaders read God-given impact manifestos.
- Churches scattered across our nation crying out for fire and impact and starting to write down their identities and objectives.
- Thousands becoming infused with effectiveness.
- The body of Christ starting to discard racism, legalism and denominationalism.
- A well of life overflowing and a shout of triumph bursting forth.

As the church rumbles to life, the Holy Spirit falls on youth graves everywhere, and the Lazarus Generation roars out, discarding drugs, perversion and violence. Then the sound of their resurrection subsides just enough for them to hear the distant roar of the revived church — the fresh-impact church! They feel drawn to that roar. We the church hear the Lazarus Generation coming forth, and we are drawn out to meet them.

Tears flow, and power unspeakable is released as God's people and the Lazarus Generation embrace.

A wall of fire reaches to the heavens and races outward to burn up a nation's sin, reducing demonic strongholds to ashes — all at the hands of a beautiful, but odd, couple.

Now you know what I mean by *Fresh Impact.*

Chapter 1
1. *Matthew Henry Commentary,* vol. 5, p. 806.
2. Ibid.
3. Ibid.

Chapter 3
1. Charles J. Sykes, *A Nation of Victims* (New York: St. Martin's Press, 1992), p. 136.
2. Ibid.

Chapter 7
1. Charles G. Finney, *How to Experience Revival* (Springdale, Penn.: Whitaker House, 1984), pp. 17-18.
2. Mario Murillo, *Fresh Fire* (Danville, Calif.: Anthony Douglas Publishing, 1991), p. 103.
3. Ibid., p. 130-131.

Chapter 12
1. I'll never forget the night I heard Burt Reynolds recount this story on the "Tonight Show" with Johnny Carson.

Chapter 14
1. Murillo, *Fresh Fire,* pp. 81-83.

Also by Mario Murillo

Fresh Fire

Fresh Fire is a guide to fresh baptisms in the Holy Spirit. There await us new drenchings of holy power — power that will more than match the flood of evil in this final moment of mankind. This book is not one more "bless-me-quick ditty." This is a book for those who want to thrive spiritually amid the insanity in these last days.

For more information about Mario Murillo's ministry or to order books, you may contact:

Mario Murillo Ministries
P.O. Box 5027
San Ramon, CA 94583
510-820-5470

If you enjoyed *Fresh Impact,* we would like to
recommend the following books:

Taking Our Cities for God
by John Dawson

This national best-seller gives you Bible-based strategies
and tactics for winning your city for God. Author John
Dawson shows you how to discover God's purpose for
your city, discern and break spiritual strongholds, and
take the five steps to victory.

There's a Miracle in Your House!
by Tommy Barnett

God wants to do something fantastic with what you
already have! This upbeat, motivating book will
revolutionize the way you think about "impossible"
situations and "overwhelming" opportunities. When
God shows you the miracle in the house, you won't
have to look anywhere else.

The House of the Lord
by Francis Frangipane

In this challenging book Francis Frangipane shows
believers how to lay aside individual difficulties and
doctrines and come together in worship and warfare—
to rebuild the house of the Lord and bring healing to
their cities.

Available at your local Christian bookstore or from:

Creation House
600 Rinehart Road
Lake Mary, FL 32746
1-800-599-5750